THE HOPE
YOU
CAN HAVE

A BOY'S JOURNEY FROM GHANA

FIFI BAIDEN

The Hope You Can Have: A Boy's Journey from Ghana
© Kingsley Baiden 2019

ISBN: 978-1-925935-66-0 (Paperback)
          978-1-925935-67-7 (eBook)

 A catalogue record for this book is available from the National Library of Australia

Editors: Peta Culverhouse and Beverley Streater
Cover Design: Ocean Reeve Publishing
Design and Typeset: Ocean Reeve Publishing
Printed in Australia by Ocean Reeve Publishing

Published by Kingsley Baiden and Ocean Reeve Publishing
www.oceanreevepublishing.com

OCEAN REEVE
PUBLISHING

I wish to dedicate this book to:

The loving memory of my late grandfather John, and my grandmother, Elizabeth:

There are no words that can fully express how I feel about your love, and I'll always thank God for putting you in my life. I'm thankful for all the extra love you showed me, and I appreciate the role you played in my early childhood.

My mother, Anna:

I appreciate everything you continue to do for me. Thank you for all the prayers and love. I love you, Mom.

My lovely wife, Kaitlynn:

Thank you for your love and constantly supporting my vision and ambition. You are my perfect wife and my best friend. I love you, always.

To all the wonderful children of the world:

I want you all to enjoy the great hope of a better future.

Foreword

In life, we all have people who inspire us towards our vision. We observe the way they do things, and we are moved to learn from them. We take the good side of them and we put away the other part of them that is not in line with our values. Ever since I joined the academy at the age of ten, I saw Tom as a visionary, a person with the desire to do whatever it took to make his vision come true. In fact, as a young boy growing up in the academy, I was moved by his passion and his determined attitude. Since day one, my relationship with Tom has been more professional than friendly. As a visionary myself, I want to inspire young children to become agents of change and Tom's work with 'Right to Dream' is something that is hard to miss.

Right to Dream founder, Tom Vernon (with permission).
'Kingsley Baiden displayed the core requirements of a Right to Dream student from day one to the highest levels. His football IQ and technical skills were at the top level for a young African player, but this, combined with his academic and social intelligence, made for a truly special human being.

The beauty of 'Right to Dream' is that a young street kerosene seller in Accra has the potential to attend a world-class university and play in Major League Soccer (MLS). Such children, like Fifi, only need guidance and opportunity and they will thrive.

Fifi was desperately unlucky with injuries and could have achieved much more in professional soccer. He was a privilege to coach and support at the academy. His achievements in the US and desire to give back to Ghana come as no surprise. In fact, I believe he has achieved only a tiny fraction of the positive impact he will have on his communities and country. Right to Dream is looking to produce leaders to take Ghana and Africa forward; Fifi is evidence that we are succeeding.'

Table of Contents

Introduction

Growing up as a child in Ghana, I experienced the negative impact of poverty. I witnessed the dissolution of many families due to poverty. I saw parents abandoning their children to escape their responsibility for taking care of them. I also observed the deaths of many children due to malnutrition and inadequate access to health care. I witnessed the death of parents who purposely committed suicide because of poverty—leaving behind many orphaned children. I was saddened by the influx of street children scattered all around the dirt roads of Accra. I observed the suffering and pain that single mothers of Ghana went through every day to put food on the table for their families.

I also noticed, with surprise, how many of the adults I had thought to be successful and self-confident, became helpless and dispirited once their social support was removed. Without jobs, money or status, they were reduced to empty shells. Yet there were a few people in Ghana like my mother and grandparents who kept their integrity and purpose despite the surrounding chaos. Their serenity was a beacon that kept others like me from losing hope. They were not necessarily the most respected, better educated, or more skilled individuals. Their composed demeanor and experience in life set me thinking: what sources of strength were they drawing on despite the economic hardship plaguing the whole nation? It is *hope*.

As hope begins to grow, it becomes contagious. The first step is to believe in yourself. Other people begin to guess what you are hoping for, and why. They start talking about you and your hope. They see what you are doing, and they want to become part of it. Yes, it attracts them. They are moved to support you to make your hope come to life. We all need support in one way or the other. Keep hoping forward. Surround yourself with people who believe in you and what you are hoping to achieve.

My HOPE is that this book inspires people to see the value in what we do and the power we have within us to bring a change to our lives and, in the world. My thoughts are born out of my personal experience throughout my life and my interaction with some inspiring people. While we all have different life experiences, I hope this book can act as a motivating tool to help you to keep your hope alive.

Kingsley 'Fifi' Baiden

The Baiden (pronounced: 'BAY-den') Family Tree

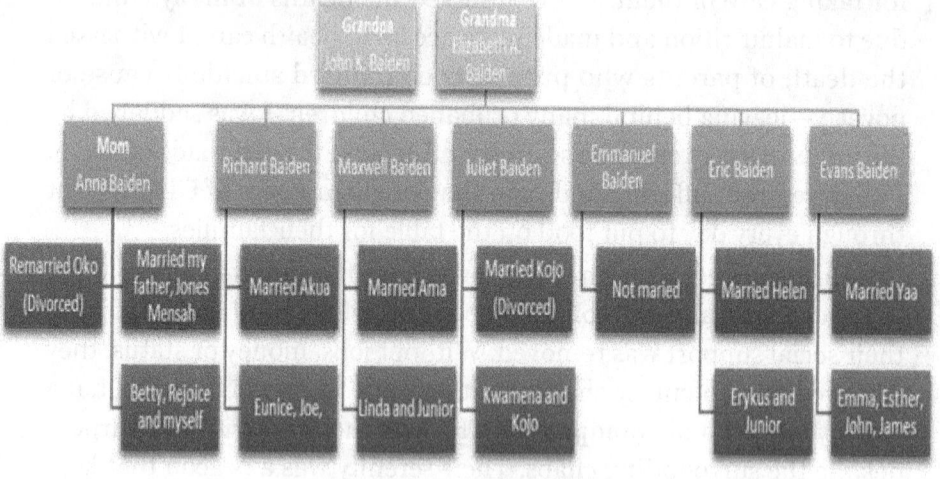

CHAPTER 1

Childhood—abandoned but not broken

Hope is being able to see that there is light despite all of the darkness
—Desmund Tutu

Life is a gift. Always appreciate what you have and be willing to share what you have—values, time, resources—with others in need. We've all heard the saying, 'when life gives you lemons, make lemonade.' This saying is what I perceive my life to be, standing at the crossroads of poverty and hope, trying to look both ways at once. My name is Kingsley Fifi Baiden. This is my life. This is my story. At this point, I'm sure some of you are wondering why I didn't go by my first real name Kingsley, instead using Fifi. Well, let me tell you: in Ghana, almost every child is given an English name. Having an English name in Ghana is more of a sign of respect to our colonizers, the British, and a symbol of our civilization. Children are also given a local Ghanaian nickname based on the day they were born. I was born on a Friday, and Fifi is one of the common local Ghanaian names for Friday-borns. There are lots of 'Fifis' in Ghana, so I wouldn't recommend going to Ghana looking for 'Fifi' because you would end up going through a lot of Fifis in just a few minutes. I guess I go by Fifi because it's easier for people to remember, but most importantly, Fifi reminds me of who I am and where I came from. It's a constant reminder of my Ghanaian heritage. So, as I said, the name is Fifi Baiden. This is my life. This is my story. Every word in this book is meant to inspire. There were many grammatical errors and the misuse of 'has' and 'have,' before I asked for assistance with editing of this story—English is my second language, after all. My first official Ghanaian language is Fante (pronounced: FAN-tea), but I also speak several other Ghanaian languages like Twi (pronounced: T-wee), and Ga (pronounced: G-ah). So, I write in English because, I want you, the reader, to focus on the big picture and see this book and its message clearly—to bring hope and to inspire people to have a positive outlook towards life.

It all started on a rainy day in Ghana. My mom was heaving and gasping with labor pain. She was rushed to the Korle Bu teaching hospital in Accra. My grandparents were anxiously pacing back and forth in the hospital halls for their grandson to be born. My father was not in sight. He was on duty somewhere at the Burma Camp Barracks. After all, he wasn't expected to be there anyway. He had abandoned us a few months before. My grandparents started praying, but the child wouldn't come out. The nurses kept urging my mother to push and push. Suddenly, she grunted and pushed, and the infant's head appeared—only the head. Finally, my mother gave a great push and I came into the world—a lovely boy with spots of black curly hair and happy brown eyes. From that very day—the day that I was born—my life's struggle began.

I had little black spots all over my skin. I guess you can call them birthmarks; a birthmark of life's struggles inherited from generations. When I look back on my early childhood, I often wonder how I survived. It was not the worst childhood, of course. Everyone talks about the woes of their early childhood, but nothing compared to its Ghanaian counterpart: malnutrition, diseases, stunted growth, and an absent father. Above all, we were very poor. I grew up knowing that life was full of uncertainties. One thing was sure, however; I knew that I had a loving extended family that I could depend on—one that I trust and that would do anything in their power to help me navigate through the world.

My father had abandoned us months before I was born. Many claimed that my father stopped loving my mom because of 'juju,' which translates to 'black magic.' My father and my mother met in my hometown in Ajumako (Ajoo-ma-koh)—a little town located in the central region of Ghana. My father enlisted to join the Ghanaian Army, and my mother was a trader at the time. She was only eighteen years old when they started dating. At first, my father loved my mother. They would be seen holding hands, cracking jokes, and showing affection to each other. They were the model of love from heaven in the small village of Ajumako. After several months of courtship, my father was posted to Burma Camp—a small police barracks in Accra—by the Ghanaian Army.

Meanwhile, my grandfather, John Kobina Baiden, and my grandmother, Elizabeth Abban Baiden, who had lived their whole life in my hometown, started to raise their family. My grandfather was a short, stout and round-faced man with a heart of gold. His words were so soothing that they could take your problems away. My grandfather stood at five feet tall, and he was very stingy about money. His stinginess would cause my uncles to refer to him as 'professor,' a nickname that would catch on to the rest of the family. Everyone started calling my grandfather 'professor,' whenever he refused to use his money to buy something for us. He would often say that he didn't have any money to share, even when he had money in his pocket. Sometimes when we walked a great distance to visit friends, he would not buy any water for us on the way and continue to tell us to keep walking and get water at home. Besides being stingy, my grandfather also had another problem; he was quick-tempered. His quick temper made us believe that all short people were quick-tempered.

My uncles were always in trouble for teasing my grandfather. My grandfather had this belt that he used to spank us. Whenever he got mad, he would be looking around for his belt; it was a black belt that most of the time hung around his small waist. My grandparents hardly fought about anything, but my grandfather's quick temper got him in trouble with my grandmother on different occasions. Many of those occasions were a quick verbal exchange between the two of them until my grandfather cooled down.

My grandmother was a warm, caring, and nurturing woman who loved her family. She stood at roughly five and a half feet tall and would always be seen busily working. She loved to work. She was always doing something—whether it was cooking, washing clothes, or cleaning the apartment. My grandmother was not your typical, conservative, obedient Ghanaian housewife. She was the breadwinner for the family.

Having grown tired of living the village life and looking for a better life for their children, my grandparents gathered all their belongings and fled to Accra (pronounced: uh-kraa) with their children. Like hundreds of Ghanaians, my grandparents left behind their occupation as farmers in the village and went to Accra for a better life.

However, life in Accra proved harder than they anticipated. There were no jobs available, and the rent was higher. My grandparents had four children at the time but eventually had three more in Accra—seven children all up. In Africa, large families are normal because of poverty. Parents give birth to eight to ten children and sometimes even more, with the hope that one day, one of their children will get them out of poverty. In many parts of Africa, where armed conflict is rampant, parents hope that at least one of their offspring will survive the conflict to protect their family name and continue the lineage.

My mother, Anna Baiden, is the eldest of them. My mother was a very beautiful, slightly- built woman standing at five feet tall, with short, coal-black, wavy hair. Her skin tone was a rich, smooth, and creamy ivory color that accented her high cheekbones and brown eyes which always seemed to sparkle. She worked hard and sacrificed her needs and dreams in life to help provide for the family.

I looked like the clone of my mother in terms of facial resemblance. Whenever we walked down the street, everyone could easily detect the family resemblance. Some people would refer to us as twins—a compliment that caused a lot of jealousy from my sisters and my younger brother. Two years younger than my mother, is my Uncle Richard Kobina—my grandparents' second-born child.

My Uncle Richard had similar qualities to my grandfather. He was also quick-tempered and only a foot taller than my grandfather. My Uncle Richard was by far the most outspoken person in the family. He was kind, but he didn't take any nonsense. He would argue and fight with people to protect his rights. He became the go-to person whenever the family encountered anyone who wanted to fight us. We would run home and call my Uncle Richard, who would often beat the person in front of everyone. He developed the reputation of being strong and someone that everyone in the area would avoid fighting.

Then my aunt, Juliet, was a five foot seven inches tall woman with an eye for beauty and fashion. She was born three years apart from my Uncle Richard. Then, two years later, they gave birth to my second uncle—Maxwell Assan. He took the facial resemblance of my grandmother. He was often with my Uncle Richard. They were either teasing my grandfather or hustling the streets of Accra to make ends meet. My Uncle Eric was born four years after my Uncle Maxwell.

My Uncle Eric became known as the 'brains of the family'. Not that any of my family members are stupid, but my Uncle Eric had a deep interest in education. He took my grandfather's features—his face, and size and his somewhat quick-tempered nature. My Uncle Eric was always reading about something and would stay up late studying and wake up late in the afternoon, especially on the weekends. He was a very neat person; some might even call him germophobic because he hated dirt or anything that breeds germs. He would wash his hands more than twenty times a day and cover his nose whenever he stepped onto the dirty roads of Accra.

My Uncle Evans was one year apart from my Uncle Eric. They looked like twins when they walked together. My Uncle Evans was a very kind person. He was very quiet in personality and humble at heart. He loved helping people and giving up his time and resources to make others happy. He was hardworking and soft-spoken. His over-generosity was mostly criticized by my grandparents because he would be gone all day working for people and he would come home empty-handed because he would work for them for free.

My Uncle Emmanuel (Emma) had the blend of both my grandparents. He was born five years after my Uncle Evans was born. My Uncle Emmanuel was quiet and soft-spoken but quick-tempered in any unjust situation. He was hardworking too, like all my family members. I spent most of my time with my Uncle Emmanuel because he was closer to my age since he was the last born of my grandparents. We were so close that we became something like 'real brothers.' Everyone in our neighborhood referred to us as brothers and often mistook me as Emma's younger brother.

When my grandparents got to Accra, they settled in a small town of Accra called Abossey Okai (Ah-bossy O-k-eye)—a hub for used auto parts businesses and hustlers, people who would do anything in their means to make money at all cost, whether it meant using sneaky or deceitful means to make money. The streets were filled with pedestrians and honking cars as they made their way to buy used auto parts for their overused cars. They rented a small one-bedroom apartment with no bathroom and no running water with the little money they had saved from their farming in the village. The ceiling was punctured with holes, causing the rain to drip through the holes whenever it rained.

My grandmother used to put a jar in the room to collect the dripping water that trickled through the holes to use as drinking water. At night, we were kept awake by the noise of the rats, running on the aluminum ceiling as they were chased by neighborhood cats. In the morning, we would find rat droppings in the drinking water in the bucket.

My grandparents divided the room with a curtain to create a bedroom and a living room. My grandparents slept in the makeshift bedroom with all their belongings crammed into that little space. My mom and uncles and aunt all slept together, packed in like sardines in a can, on the living room floor on the thin cloth that was spread out by my grandmother. Sleeping on the cloth felt like sleeping on a sheet of newspaper. They did all the cooking outside of the apartment in a small coal-pot. This old-fashioned coal-pot produced dense smoke that filled the air, causing anyone nearby to cough their lungs out. The coal-pot was so rickety that sometimes the boiling water or soup slopped down the sides of the coal-pot, scalding my grandmother, or toddlers if they accidentally bumped into it.

The apartment they rented was a compound house with about seven single bedroom apartments. Unfortunately, Ghanaians have large families, with each family having about five or more children. Walking into the apartment complex felt like being at a stadium or a circus with children running everywhere and parents cooking outside of their apartments. Everywhere in the apartments would smell like the fusion of savory Ghanaian food and charred wood from the cooking. Most Ghanaian foods are mostly prepared with fish, vegetables and spices that give off a strong aroma that can be deemed 'stinky' by people unfamiliar with the smell. Like a giant spider web, lines of drying clothes ran from one apartment to another. Flies, garbage, sewage, and mosquitoes were everywhere. The neighborhood children sometimes defecated in plastic bags at night and then, disposed of them by throwing them out, far into the distance—popularly called 'flying toilets'—that would make a loud sound as they landed on the aluminum roofing sheets. Life was hard and smelly; it was scary and depressing. You would see young children crowded in the dirt—young people who saw no hope and had given up.

Most unemployed adults in the neighborhood hung out in the street corners, drunk into a stupor. Life at the time was dreary, tedious, and depressing. Watching their children die of malaria, cholera, tuberculosis and other deadly diseases; struggling to pay the rent; or put a meal on the table for their families; most adults who had lost all hope found comfort in drinking alcohol or what the locals call it, akpeteshie (pronounced: ak-pet-er-she). Indeed, when in poverty, most people in Ghana were locked in a trajectory of hopelessness.

My grandfather soon found work opportunities hard to come by in Accra. My grandmother thought about starting a farming business in Accra but realized they didn't have access to a refrigerator to prolong the longevity of the farm products before they went bad. My grandfather eventually took a job as a security guard at a factory. The pay wasn't great, but it was enough to pay almost all their rent for the month. Also, my grandfather's honesty was well-praised by his boss, and he hoped to get a promotion. However, he was resented by many of the workers who wanted to steal things from the factory. They later conspired against him, causing my grandfather to seek early retirement at the age of fifty in fear for his life. Due to that poor work experience and the economic hardship of Ghana, my grandfather never returned to work again. He relied on his twenty Ghana Cedis (pronounced: Cee-dis) which is equivalent to a five-dollar monthly pension and became a stay-at-home father who spent most of his time supporting my grandmother and sharing part of his wisdom with us through his storytelling.

My grandmother in the meantime was a trader. She worked tirelessly to provide for the family. She sold used plastic bottles and jars. On Saturday mornings, my grandparents, as well as my uncles, would go to the people that picked empty plastic bottles from industrial areas and from dumpsters and buy from them. They would come home and use hot water and other disinfectants to wash and clean them. Then they would arrange them into sacks to be transported to the market. Around 3 am on Mondays, my grandmother and my uncles would carry the packed sacks of clean plastic bottles and gallons on their heads, walking about six miles to a marketplace called Nkrumah (pronounced: unh n-kroo-muh) Circle.

This busy intersection is one of the six traffic interchanges throughout Accra named after the founding fathers of Ghana, commonly known as the 'Big Six'. These included Ako Adjei (pronounced: A-ko-Ad-jay), Akufo Addo (A-coo-pho- A-do), Boakye Danquah (bo-achi, dan-quah) Kwame Nkrumah (kwa-mee unh n-kroo-muh), Obetsebi Lamptey (obey-chey-be lamp-tay) and Ofori Atta (off-oree at-tar). A statue of Dr Nkrumah, Ghana's first president and founding father of pan-Africanism, situated in an elaborate water-fountain park, represents the growth and rapid development of the nation. 'Circle,' as the locals call it, is a sprawling hub for vendors selling clothes, shoes, electronics, and people carrying goods on their heads to sell to walking pedestrians. 'Circle' is not only a marketplace but a hub for Ghana's transportation system ranging from taxis to trotros (pronounced: traw-traw) which are old cargo transport vans, Frankensteined into consumer buses by adding locally-made seats. These ubiquitous minivans with drivers' assistants, or 'mates' as the locals call them, are young men shouting the names of stops from the side window, banging the exterior to make the driver stop when he makes eye contact with a waiting passenger on the side of the road. Despite their unpleasant appearance, trotros are very safe to drive and serve as the main means of transport for many Ghanaians. There are Okadas, motorbikes that zip through the city's streets as cars crawl through the traffic. Then we have the government-owned and operated Metro Mass Transit, popularly known Kuffour buses after the president who introduced them in 2006.

My grandmother didn't sell the bottles at the 'Circle,' though, because of the low market for it. She would get a trotro or a Metro bus from 'Circle' to a big marketplace called Asamankese (pronounced: ay-sa-man-ke-see)—about two hours from Accra. She would be gone for a few days selling the plastic bottles and gallons, returning on Thursday evening with groceries for the rest of the week. We all looked forward to her arrival, because she would get us treats, and I loved her for that. The extra money was used to pay the rent of their one bedroom. She rested on Friday and repeated the same cycle again on Saturday. My grandmother was a very hard worker, never complained about work, and defied all the odds about being an uneducated Ghanaian woman.

She used to tell me that, 'life in this world is hard, especially living here in Ghana, but you have to put in the effort for God to bless you for it.'

Those words really inspired and helped me to appreciate hard work. When we put our mind and heart into something, we must back it up with our actions. Hard work is truly a prerequisite for a better life. Like most strong Ghanaian women, my grandmother defied the status quo of being confined to the house while the husbands worked.

My grandmother was the breadwinner of the house while my grandfather was the stay-at-home-father type. The truth is, my grandfather was a very hard worker as well, but he was traumatized by his working experience. He shared his wisdom with us, for which I will forever be grateful for in my life. His stories were very entertaining, yet so inspiring and often caused me to ponder over their deeper meanings throughout the day.

My mother was the eldest of the children. She started helping as a caterer when the family moved from the village to Accra and then she moved on to become a typist with the middle school education she got. She worked as a typist until she lost the job for reasons unknown. She was later drawn into selling earrings by my Aunt Juliet. My mother worked selling earrings to support my grandparents as well.

My Uncles Richard, Maxwell, Eric, Evans, and Emmanuel were all hardworking too. My Uncles Richard and Maxwell both used to sell necklaces and belts at one of Ghana's popular marketplace, Kantamanto (pronounced: Ca-tar-man-to) Market. Kantamanto is Ghana's biggest second-hand clothes market, and it is right in the heart of the capital, Accra; annexed to Makola Market, the largest point of trade in the city. Kantamanto is a community on its own—full of arrangements of hand-me-down clothes, vehicle spare parts, home décor, and footwear, which together give it the look of a grand flea market with almost no space left to spare. Sometimes bells ring out, and at other times whole choruses are improvised to attract buyers. Shoppers comb through clothes on hangers and shoes dangling by their laces. The less attractive products usually find their way onto the floor, in heaps that are known locally as the 'bend-down boutique.' Market activity starts very early in the morning, so latecomers get the floor offerings and other leftovers. Locals call second hand clothes 'obroni we wu '(pronounced: oh-bro-knee-way-wu), meaning 'the white person has died,' as that seems the most likely reason for their belongings being put back on the market. In Ghana, your hand-me-down clothes go to the family, but since every white is perceived to be rich and have more clothes, their hand-me-down clothes end up on the market.

My Uncles Richard and Maxwell would leave very early in the morning to make their way to Kantamanto Market to compete over customers with the many necklace and belt sellers in the market.

They were very aggressive and smart about the way they attracted customers to purchase their goods. My Aunt Juliet sold earrings and makeup on the market. She was really into beauty and cosmetics. She would be gone for hours selling these things to Ghanaian women aspiring to be Ghana's next top models. My Uncle Eric was the book-smart type. He won a scholarship to one of Ghana's finest high schools, Accra Academy, and studied science. He was often seen reading and researching about topics such as diversity and freedom.

My Uncle Evans, on the other hand, was a carpenter. Like Richard and Maxwell, he was also very hardworking. With no formal education beyond the middle school level, he became an apprentice to a carpenter in our area and learned the trade. He became one of the best carpenters in the neighborhood. I used to help my Uncle Evans when I was around the age of six. I would hold his plywood down for him to mark with his pencil, which was always placed in his front pocket before he would use his handsaw to cut the measured wood to make a table or chair. I used to ask him so many questions about his work and he loved working with me because I always offered to help. I remember being impressed by my Uncle Evans' focus on his carpentry.

I thought his sense of design was pretty good because he knew how to make things with any wood. He made the chairs in my grandparents' room and fixed the windows as well. On some occasions, I would help him make a couple of tables and chairs for me to sell in our neighborhood. I loved selling the chairs and tables because I took a lot of pride in them since I helped him make them. My Uncle Evans took a lot of time though to make sure every inch of a table or chair was done right and even the parts like under the tables or chairs that people couldn't see.

'Why do you spend so much time on your work, uncle?' I asked him one day.

'You know, what you do is who you are. Make sure you do everything with all your might,' he replied with a big smile on his face. My Uncle Evans' desire to work hard and doing things with so much focus left a lasting impression on me.

My Uncle, Emmanuel (or Emma, as we called him), had a passion for soccer. He was very good at it. I used to carry his backpack containing his soccer shoes to the field for him. I used to kick around with Emma and his friends since the age of three. They pushed me off the ball, they kicked me, and they smacked the ball at my face many times because I stayed in the goal. I would cry and cry to get them in trouble, but I always begged them to play with me again. I started accompanying Emma to his club soccer games, I was about five years old. He played for a local team called Rot Weiss (pronounced: root-wise).

I went to several home games at Rot Weiss with Emma and my love for the sport started to grow quickly. Emma and his passion for soccer was one example of the many Ghanaians who dedicated their time to playing soccer in the hope of using soccer to make it out of poverty. Emma was very good at soccer and dreamt of playing soccer at the professional level overseas. For me though, soccer at the age of six years old was just a fun activity for me to do with Emma. I continued to make it a priority to play with Emma because soccer offered me a sense of freedom and fun—a break from worrying about the daily demands of poverty. It helped Emma and me to bond together and develop a very close relationship. Our relationship was made possible because of our closeness in age. Emma and I are only two years apart, and so we spent a lot of time playing soccer together. Our relationship grew from uncle/cousin relationship to become like real brothers.

My uncles and my aunt were all hard workers who labored every day to support my grandparents. All nine of them were crammed in that small apartment my grandparents rented, with all their belongings. You can imagine how cramped it was. At night, they would stack the furniture in the room to make space to sleep and then with no space between them. Things did not get better after that. My grandparents refused to return to the village because although the city life was filled with bills, they were able to have better access to hospitals and education for their children compared to the village.

Going back to the village also meant that they failed at life and wouldn't be able to face the shame from people in the village. Whatever the reasons may be, my grandparents were not ready to move back to the village life with their growing family. As my grandparents' children all got older, my mother married my father and left with him. My Uncle Richard also got married to Akua (ay-coo-huh), and moved to Mallam, a crowded place where he still lives. They now had four children—Eunice, Daddy Joe, Lizzy, and Efua (ey-foo-ah). My Uncle Maxwell also married Ama, a sweet lady, and moved to Winneba and they had two children, Linda and Junior.

My Uncle Eric got a teaching job at a middle school in Obuasi and moved. My Aunt Juliet got married to Bro Kojo and they moved to a town called Russia, where they ended up having two children, Kwamena and Kojo shaki. At this point, my mother, my Aunt Juliet, and my Uncles Richard, Maxwell, and Eric had all moved from the apartment and went on to live with their husbands or wives except for my Uncles Evans and Emmanuel. My grandparents began to suffer financially as they lost the little income they received from my mom, my uncles and my aunt.

Not too long after they moved, my grandmother was diagnosed with a rare disease impacting her spinal cord. She was crippled in bed for many months. She had to be in an orthopedic cast—from the top of her chest down to her waist—for six months. Her unexpected spinal disease was linked to the witchcraft of her own sisters.

Witchcraft is a cultural reality in Ghana, regardless of any scientific stance on its validity. Women are easy targets of witchcraft—especially older ones or widows who are not protected by men any more, or those who share the same husband. Like most sub-Saharan countries, Ghana is one of the most religious countries with its colorful mixture of Christians, Muslims, and traditional/ancestral worshippers, or Animalists. Despite the advances in technology and education, witchcraft is still prevalent in Ghana to the point where they have witch camps to isolate labelled witches. Like many African countries, colonization led us to find meanings behind any disaster. They took our resources, enslaved our men and women, and left us in extreme poverty and no meaning of life.

Witchcraft can be broadly referred to as 'the ability to harm someone by means of mystical power'. Like fate, irony, luck, and karma, it addresses the 'why' behind misfortunes, as opposed to the 'how.' Why did this person die at a young age? Why was this child struck by the falling coconut? Why did this man become an alcoholic? While people from Western cultures would attribute these things to luck, karma, fate or lack of resources, some Ghanaians would look for an explanation from fake prophets or some human agency.

According to several pastors, my grandmother's sisters in the village became jealous of my grandmother because they assumed that she was having success in Accra. The pastors said they felt that my grandmother's children were all working to generate money in the city. So, they both decided to cast a spell on my grandmother with the goal that if she died, her children would return to the village to help them financially or even take them to the city to enjoy the city life. Whether this revelation was true or not, my grandmother's sisters came to the hospital and confessed their witchcraft in front of everyone.

Both sisters were crying uncontrollably as they begged my grandmother for forgiveness. I forgot to mention that my grandparents were very religious. Like most Ghanaian families, religion was the safe haven that brought meaning to many people's lives amid the poverty that plagued my country. My grandfather started as a member of the Methodist Church but later became a Jehovah's Witness. My grandmother, on the other hand, was a member of the Assemblies of God Church. Despite their religious differences, my grandparents allowed their children to make the decision of which religion they would want to affiliate themselves with.

On Sundays, my grandparents would dress in their finest clothes and make their way to their different churches. My mom, uncles, and aunt all went with my mom to the Assemblies of God Church on Sundays. My grandfather was usually alone. On Christmas day, my grandmother would make the most delicious meal in celebration of the occasion. My grandfather would refuse to eat the 'Christmas meal' that my grandmother prepared, as the Christmas celebration is not acceptable among Jehovah's Witnesses. They saw Christmas as a pagan ritual, with no real evidence of December 25 being the correct date of birth of Jesus Christ.

Whether this is true or not, my grandfather did not dare to eat the meal. I began to suspect that my mom, my uncles, and aunt all went with my grandmother because of the 'special meal' they got to eat on their birthdays and during Christmas.

When I lived with my grandparents, I was also given the choice to go with my grandmother or grandfather. I loved them both dearly, and I always thought that they had a unique love between them despite their different religious beliefs. On Sundays, I would alternate going to church with my grandmother or my grandfather. I was often eager to go with my grandmother because I got to have some treats like candy or crackers that they gave us at Sunday School.

They didn't have any treats at my grandfather's Jehovah's Witness church, and so I often felt reluctant to go with my grandfather. I was the only member of the family that volunteered to go with my grandfather, a decision I was often teased about by my grandmother and peers. Most of my peers saw Jehovah's Witnesses as too restricting and often mocked me for associating myself with them. Despite the excruciating embarrassment among my peers, I was determined to hold on to my vow of going to church with both my grandmother and grandfather.

I was drawn to the fact that most people at the grandfather's Jehovah's Witness church wore a suit and a tie. I often wondered how they had the money to buy their suit. Whatever the reason, I liked how neatly dressed they were and how they all had discussions instead of listening to a preacher the whole time. To be honest, I began to be torn in faith. Although both churches preached that God is the supreme being and He sent His son to die for our sins, they had different beliefs or rituals.

At my grandfather's Jehovah's Witness church, they use the name 'Jehovah' a lot.

'Grandpa, who is" Jehovah"? Is that your pastor's name?' I asked him after church one day. He smiled and said, 'Good question Fifi. Jehovah is God's name.' For a five-year-old, knowing God's name was like finally solving an ancient Chinese puzzle in my heart.

My grandmother's church only referred to God by 'Lord'. It didn't sound as cool as Jehovah, but I still accepted it like any five-year-old would do.

Another difference that I noticed other than birthday and Christmas celebrations was the notion of heaven and hell. At the Sunday school at my grandmother's church, they told us that when you do good, you will go to heaven and when you do bad, you will go to hell. The word, 'hell', became one of my least favorite words.

'Pastor, please would I go to heaven?' I asked the head of the Sunday children's school after one of our meetings. He looked at me with a faint smile, 'Yes Fifi, only if you do good. Be good okay?' he said.

I nodded and ran to hold my grandmother. On the other hand, my grandfather's church told me that there was no hell.

It was all very confusing to me, but what I liked the most about this whole experience was seeing my grandparents live happily despite their differences in faith. Also, I like that they gave their children and their grandchildren like myself the option to choose which religion we would affiliate ourselves with. I concluded in my heart that God is the source of love. Anyway, as a believer in God, my grandmother embraced the Bible's message on forgiveness.

'If you forgive others of their trespasses then your Heavenly Father will also forgive you of your many sins: But if you don't forgive others of their trespasses, neither will your Father forgive your trespasses,' the Bible states at Matthew 6:14.

Not surprisingly, my grandmother did indeed forgive her sisters. The rest of her life would be about recovery and physical therapy to slowly remove the physical and psychological trauma of being in bed for almost a year without any movement. She was barred from lifting anything heavy or sitting down for a long time.

The whole family became very disoriented after the doctor told my grandmother to abstain from work. She walked with a cane for a very long time, and she continued to go to the hospital once a month for a check-up. So, the breadwinner was down, and this was a major blow to the family's financial status. Despite this significant hit, the family remained calm and maintained hope in the face of adversity.

Not too long after the fall of my grandmother, my mother's marriage failed, and she divorced my biological father. Unlike in the United States and other western cultures where there is alimony to protect women, Ghana did not have that in its legal system. As a result, my mother and her children moved back to stay in the same apartment with my grandparents and my uncles. Almost like a plan or coincidence, my sister Juliet, also came running in tears to settle in the same apartment with her children after a terrible divorce with her husband.

Now the little apartment, which housed my grandparents and her seven children, was a hub for my grandparents, my two uncles, two single mothers, and five grandchildren. At this point, life became very challenging. Having three square meals a day was a real struggle and education was not even considered to be the focus. Sometimes we had to go to bed on empty stomachs or I would go and beg our neighbors for food.

Amid this chaos, the blue sky was my only hope of a better life. Every day I would look up the sky and constantly remind myself that even though there was rain and thunderstorms, there was always a beautiful blue sky with birds flapping their wings. I always used the blue sky as a reminder of hope and kept my peace. We all had to play a role to support the family, whether it was selling earrings, furniture, iced water, or kerosene.

CHAPTER 2

Prophecy: Is it fulfilled?

Dream lofty dreams, and as you dream, so you shall become. Your vision is the promise of what you shall one day be; your ideal is the prophecy of what you shall at last unveil—James Allen

The only times my grandparents went back to visit our hometown, Ajumako, was to either visit family members or attend a funeral. Most times, however, they visited because of the annual festival. I love the festivals in Ghana as they are part of the rich culture established in the country. Ghana is divided into ten regions: Greater Accra, Ashanti, Central, Eastern, Northern, Western, Upper East, Upper West, Brong Ahafo and Volta. All these regions have their distinct language or dialect, and their own festival. Ghana's festivals are one of the country's most attractive features. They reveal a lot about the art and culture of Ghana, the beliefs, and common features of the Ghanaian society. The festivals and the ceremonies are very colorful and reflect the rich diversity of history and culture of tribal life in the respective regions.

These festivals also present a wonderful opportunity for people to remember their ancestors and to bond. Ajumako is in the central region of Ghana and proudly celebrates the Akwambo festival. Akwambo is observed annually, but mainly in the central region of Ghana. Celebrations are held at various times of the year, usually lasting for several days, and can include different activities according to local customs.

The Akwambo festival shares certain common customs such as the ritual path clearing, durbar, offerings, and family or community reunions. There may also be music and dance performances, soccer games, and parades. In some areas, young people hold an all-night party. Path clearing is perhaps the most important part of Akwambo festival. It is a ritual honoring the first settlers who established the town. Every member of the community is expected to participate in clearing the paths and roads leading to the town, as well as those that provide access to streams, rivers, farms, shrines, and communal spaces. Unpaved footpaths are weeded and maintained, while paved roads are ritually swept with branches, brooms, and fans made of leaves.

During the Akwambo festivals, we see the community leaders and chiefs being carried around the dusty village by a group of strong men. Although the village is poor, the chiefs and queens wear gold ornaments and are shaded by a huge umbrella. I often wondered why the people would waste their gold on the chiefs and queens instead of using that to help improve the village. I asked my grandmother about this, and she explained that it is part of tradition.

'It doesn't make sense to me, grandma,' I remarked.

'Tradition is tradition, and we can do nothing to change what has been passed down to us,' my grandmother interjected, sensing that I was getting annoyed.

'They should sell the gold to improve the village and provide hospital and jobs for the people instead of covering the chiefs and queens with them,' I concluded.

Our desire to preserve our African culture and traditions placed us on the opposite end of the rest of the world, and we continue to play catch up today.

After a few hours of ostentatiously parading the chiefs and queens of the village, with echoes of drumming and voices of singers filled the air, the community leaders would now pay respect to the ancestors. These ancestors are perceived to be spirits serving as mediators between the people and God. They pour wine or scatter food on the ground and usher words to the ancestors in the hope of providing protection, good fortune, and blessings in the form of rain and successful harvests.

The people at the festival are decorated in the traditional kente (pronounced: ken-tey) cloths. These kente cloths are colored pattern cloth strips that are woven by hand. The drummers continuously play traditional Ghanaian music that is too loud for the ears but has the power to move everyone to dance. Next to the drummers are the traditional warriors discharging muskets as they dance rhythmically to the music and cheered by the people. Children run around happily chasing the goats and sheep, leaving behind them a big cloud of dust. You can smell the smoke coming out from all corners of the village as people prepare their favorite dish in celebration of the festival. All the people seem to be in good moods as they lend a helping hand to their neighbors. The whole scene looks like a sea of rainbow colors covering beautiful people of all ages. Everyone looks very happy. The small village barely has one hundred people in it but during the festival, thousands of people, including foreigners, travel long distances, from all over the country, to witness the Akwambo festival.

My grandparents would gather all of us from Accra to attend the festival where we spent about one week in Ajumako before going back to Accra. I was very popular in Ajumako during the annual Akwambo festival because of my unique appearance. When I was born, my mother said everybody loved me—I mean, who wouldn't, right? My mom said people loved me because of my skin color. Unlike most Ghanaians, I was fair in complexion. During the Akwanbo festival, my popularity skyrocketed. People would stop and ask why my hair was so soft and why my skin was so light.

People believed that I was a white boy, and they started calling me 'obroni (oh-bro-knee),' directly translated to 'white boy.' My mother also started calling me 'mi obroni,'—my white boy. According to my mother, people would request her to bring me to the Akwanbo festival in our hometown because they wanted to see the only obroni baby among the sea of black Ghanaian children and adults.

One day at the festival, while I was being paraded through the village, a very tall man approached my mom. Standing at about six feet five inches tall, the man could easily be identified in the village. He was also a Muslim, in fact, the only Muslim in the whole village of Ajumako. Nobody knew how he ended up in the village, but he gained everyone's approval and the whole village loved him. He would often be seen laughing with people or offering deep advice to others.

'Take really good care of the boy,' he said, as he looked at me curiously.

'Yes, I will,' my mom sincerely replied.

'This boy is special. He's not from here. He's a foreigner. Take really good care of him,' the man said.

At this point, my mom was surprised to hear those strong words. In fact, she was later to claim that this was a prophecy. 'Okay, I will. Thank you!' my mom replied, with a smile of bewilderment.

My mother thought to herself, My little boy is not Ghanaian? He's a foreigner? How could this be? She told me that she pondered a lot about what the man said. The secret about me being an 'obroni' was finally out. I was indeed not a Ghanaian, I was a foreigner—a boy who just came in flesh to Ghana, but in spirit, I was a stranger. My mother tells this story of the prophecy with such vividness and belief.

When I was in Ghana in the summer of 2018, my mother told me the story again. She even said to me that if the man was still alive, she would've asked me to go and see the man in Ajumako. My mom's belief in this prophecy led to me thinking about an encounter that I had at school many years ago.

My school, Abossey Okai Elementary, was a low-slung old cement building about two miles from my house. Even before I started elementary school, I had learned how to read a little bit from the newspaper and building signs. Unlike many Ghanaian children, my keen interest in learning gave me a jump-start towards excelling in the classroom.

All the teachers I had in school really liked me for my quiet personality and attention in class. I think I was in first or second grade when I had a teacher called Mrs. Deborah Attah. She liked me ever since I had joined her class. She admired my attentiveness in class and my desire to work hard and learn. She often called on me to answer questions in class which I did with ease. 'Great job, Kingsley,' she would often say with a big smile on her face. In my class, it looked like it was just me that she cared about.

All my classmates knew that I was one of the most studious pupils in class because whenever the teacher asked a general question, they would turn their heads toward my direction. They would all give me a big round of applause, beating the top of the worn-out wooden desks that separated our sardine-like arrangement in the small classroom. One day after the bell rang for the close of school, Mrs. Deborah asked me to wait behind.

'I want to talk to you Kingsley, wait behind,' she said to me without making eye contact as she continued writing some report.

'Okay,' I said and started to put away my three pieces of white chalk, my little chalkboard, and the broken pencil on my desk.

After the classroom was empty, she cleared her throat and said, 'I want you to tell your mom that I want to adopt you as my son. You have a bright future and I want to give you the best education.'

I nodded and said, 'Okay, I will tell her.'

As she was leaving through the door, she looked back at me and said, 'Let me know what your mother says, okay?' Again, I nodded without saying a word. 'Bye Kingsley,' she added before disappearing through the doorway.

I was a little confused on my way home, thinking about what she meant by adoption and whether I would ever see my family again. I arrived home, my mind confused and excited likewise. I greeted my grandparents and quickly asked for my mom.

'She went out to sell her earrings. She should be back soon,' my grandmother said.

'I have some news for her. I mean, my teacher told me to tell her something,' I said to my grandmother.

'What is it?' my grandmother asked, with a hint of nervousness in her voice. As I was about to tell her, my mom walked in, carrying the box of her earrings on her head. She looked very tired.

'Mom, my teacher asked me to tell you something,' I blurted out, as she set the box on the cement floor.

'What is it obroni? Did something happen at school?' She faced me, concerned and curious.

'My teacher, Mrs. Deborah told me to tell you that she wants to adopt me,' I replied.

She was taken back and didn't know what to say. 'Why does she want to adopt you?' my grandmother interjected.

'She said I have a bright future and that she wants to give me the best education.' I said quickly.

'That's very nice of her but tell her we can't give you up for adoption,' my mom said graciously.

'Yes, I agree with your mother, we are not going to give you up for adoption. We all love you Fifi,' my grandmother said with tears in her eyes.

'Okay, I will let her know,' I replied and departed to go play outside with my friends in the neighborhood.

As I reflected on this part of my childhood, I questioned a few things. Did my mom refuse to give me up for adoption because she thought I was special? Was it because of the prophecy? The next day, I went to school and relayed the message to my teacher. She seemed very disappointed about the response she received, but she replied, 'Okay Kingsley, I understand. Thank you for telling me.' I think Mrs. Deborah saw something in me.

It was not merely my intelligence but something bigger. Perhaps she saw the prophecy as well? Either way, she continued to call on me and helped me to improve on my English. Mrs. Deborah will always hold a special place in my heart as one of my favorite teachers of all time.

My mom still calls me 'obroni,' even though my skin is darker than hers. I believe she calls me that, not because of my skin color, but because of the prophecy that she received about me. She believed it then, and she still does. In fact, my whole family believes it. After much convincing, I think I do too. After all, words are as powerful as a sword; they can build up or tear down. What we say has the power to become or not to become. In my case, those words were a sign of hope for my family. Our actions need to align with our words, though. The tall Muslim man gave the prophecy, but the rest of it was part of my journey. I ended up in America to live my dream. I may be a Ghanaian by birth, but to my mom, I'm still her 'obroni' or little white boy.

CHAPTER 3

Kerosene seller

If we expect change, we must act on our hope every day until we have accomplished what we wanted—Christopher Goodman

Everything in Africa comes down to money. Many of Africa's problems stem from poverty and its declining standard of living. Poverty is widespread and many people are engulfed in a 'poverty trap' of despair and hopelessness. There is a constant yearning for a happier life despite how farfetched it may seem for many Ghanaians. It is the long-term poverty that has been transmitted from one generation to the next. As families struggle to make ends meet, parents are forced to use every resource they have to survive—including their children.

In Ghana, on any given day, in any given region, one can find children performing different tasks either by their own ingenuities or based on the instructions of their parents. Children carry baskets and trays on their heads in the loud, hot and bustling market—a far cry from the comfortable, air-conditioned grocery stores in the US. Children also hawk vegetables, iced water, fruit, plantain, smoked fish, and more, on nearby street corners. As cars drive by, smoke and dust kick up and fill their nostrils, covering their whole body, while beads of sweat trickle down their foreheads.

In the domestic environment, children take on duties ranging from the fetching of water, pounding of fufu (pronounced: phoo-phoo), a staple food made by mixing cassava and plantain, cooking, cleaning the house and so on. Children are not exempt from the hard labor that comprises agricultural responsibilities. They frequently accompany their parents to the farm, clearing the land, weeding, planting crops, searching for firewood and uprooting. Most children also help in the running of their family shop, if their parents have one. Due to the commitment of these jobs, children miss out on education and spend most of their time helping their families to survive the economy of Ghana.

Some parents give their children the option of helping them out in the market or going to school; but if they choose to go to school, when they come home, there will be no food. Due to poverty, some parents are not able to pay for exercise books, uniforms or exam fees. This forces the children to miss weeks of school and even drop out to avoid the embarrassment of being asked to leave when they can't pay the fees. I missed so many school attendances because of lack of money to pay for my exam fees. I remember a particular time: I was in fourth grade, and my grandparents didn't have the money to pay for my exam fees. When I got to school that day, the school gave me three weeks to come up with the exam fees. I failed to do so, and they spanked me six lashes on my backside. I was asked to leave school and return when I had the money in full.

Other than losing out on education, there were dangers that come with selling things on the streets and on the market. Some children were injured, raped or even died from oncoming cars as they tried to attend to customers.

In Ghana, there are many people selling the same things. Customers yell out what they want, causing a foot race between sellers racing from different directions. I usually got the upper hand because of my speed learned through soccer practice, but I lost some races to those longer-legged sellers. For example, a thirsty customer looking for some cold water would yell out, 'meto nsuo'(pronounced: me-thor—in-su-oh), or, 'I want to buy water.' Ice water sellers ran at top speed to get to the call. Unfortunately, some children tripped on loose rocks and injured their ankle or knee. Others forgot to check different directions to cross the street and were hit by oncoming cars coming at top speed. Sadly, some children were also lured into homes of pedophiles and were raped.

I have fallen many times when selling on the streets. I had a car run over my foot one time but luckily, it was a slow-moving car in traffic and wasn't coming at top speed, so the damage to my foot wasn't bad.

Despite the danger, children's work could be described as a survival strategy for many families and even had a contractual meaning. Children received a lot from their parents in terms of food, clothes, expenditure on their education and the right to inheritance in the future; children were, therefore, expected to reciprocate support from parents by contributing their labor. Historically, parents and guardians expected children to contribute to household chores such as cooking, washing, child-minding, petty trading and so on. Among many Ghanaian adults, children are economic assets of their families, who must contribute in different ways to improve their own wellbeing and that of their families. Children are trained to perpetuate the existence of their families and cultural legacies. Traditionally, from about the age of seven and in some cases even six, children in Ghana are expected to participate in the adult world of work. Boys are expected to engage in manual types of work while girls follow their mothers mainly at domestic chores. Work, especially within the family, is seen as something positive for a child's future and the children themselves see it as something good for them. In lieu of this, the family and the community as whole join hands to inculcate this vision into children and young people. So, children contribute significantly to the livelihoods of their families. In Ghana, children are active agents in unpaid household work—an enterprise where parents rely greatly on their services. Most children miss a lot of school attendance or become dropouts because of economic reasons. For many Ghanaian children, it comes down to their parents giving them a choice of eating or going to school to learn and play with friends.

At the age of seven, I sold kerosene to help my family survive. Kerosene, an energy-efficient oil, has been used as a good source of heat for decades. This is due to the simplicity, quality, and cost. Kerosene heaters and oil cost much less than propane or other heating fuels, and unlike wood or coal, you need much less kerosene to provide the same amount of energy. As one of the most essential petroleum products in Ghana, kerosene is used extensively in both rural and urban areas for cooking and lighting up the house and the marketplace at night with lanterns and other equipment. Kerosene only needs a match or spark to ignite, meaning it works without any electricity.

In Ghana, many kerosene sellers peddle their wares in the evening at dusk, when most people purchase fuel for their lamps. So, I carried my kerosene to soccer practice at Rot Weiss so I could sell it in the marketplace after practice on the way home. Despite daily profit only amounting to two or three US dollars, the kerosene business was a very lucrative in Ghana because of its widespread use. Almost every home-made use of kerosene in one way or the other, and people experienced hardship whenever kerosene went scarce.

I would miss school sometimes to get in long lines to purchase kerosene at the gas station to sell on the market. I used to borrow some money from some of our neighbors to buy two gallons of kerosene costing about four US dollars I'd paid them their full amount back with a little bit of interest after I'd sold all the kerosene. I used a funnel and cola bottles to measure and serve my kerosene to customers, using the two contour horizontal lines of the bottle to differentiate when people requested a quarter, a half or a full bottle of kerosene. During our school vacations, I would sell chairs made by my Uncle Evans during the day and then kerosene in the evening after practice to support my family.

Kerosene was my main business because it generated the most money to help my family. But selling kerosene has its ups and downs: on the good days, I would sell all my kerosene and generate enough profit to provide groceries for the family for a few days. However, on the bad days, I would trip and spill all my kerosene and go home empty handed. It is usually the bad days that I remember the most.

The first time I had a bad day selling kerosene was when I slipped and broke all my bottles. It was a rainy day in Accra. The rain kept us in our congested little room—our hope, our strength, our only dry place. School and soccer practice were cancelled that day because of the rain. The ground was very muddy. We had breakfast—bread with water. As we ate the bread hungrily, we wondered when the rain would stop. My grandfather went into one of his storytelling modes, and we listened attentively, laughing uncontrollably at the funniest parts. We didn't have money for dinner that day, but I had some kerosene left in the gallon to sell at the Kaneshie Market. It rained all morning and throughout the afternoon.

Around 6 pm, the rain stopped, and I decided to go and sell the kerosene to help put some dinner on the table for us. Throughout my journey to the market, the ground was very muddy, as I cautiously tiptoed around puddles of water on the potholed roads of Accra to avoid slipping. When I got to the market, the place looked as lively as ever. I was surprised to see so many sellers out despite the rain. I checked my usual customers; two of them did not make it out that evening but I was able to serve the rest of my loyal customers.

One of my loyal customers, Mama Esi (pronounced: ay-see), was a five-foot-tall, strong-willed tomato seller with grey hair sticking out on the side of her head. She was about fifty-five years old and had been my customer for over two years when I first started selling kerosene at the age of seven. She fell in love with my honesty when she once accidentally dropped money on the floor, and I returned the money to her. It was about $50 at the time, a huge sum of money for any Ghanaian. She thanked me greatly for not running away with the money and giving it back to her. She mentioned that the money was meant to pay for her rent the next day. Since then, Mama Esi was my most loyal customer who would wait for hours to buy kerosene from me. I often felt bad on the days that I didn't make it to the market because I was sick. She would tell me the next time she saw me that she had to wait for a few hours before buying from another kerosene seller, and even that, she always felt as if she had betrayed me. We didn't have cell phones at the time, so there was no way for us to communicate in the days that I didn't make it out to the market.

'It's okay Mama Esi. You can buy from other kerosene customers when I don't make it out,' I would reassure her.

'Okay, but I will wait until 9 pm before I would buy from anyone,' she would reply.

I usually got to the market around 6 pm or 6:30 pm after practice. Mama Esi would wait three extra hours before she would buy from any other kerosene seller. What a great woman she was!

'Fifi, what took you so long?' Mama Esi asked, when she caught sight of me. It was around 7.30 pm.

'It was the rain, Mama Esi. I didn't leave my house until around 6:30 pm,' I replied with a smile on my face.

'Give me the usual,' she responded.

Her usual was full bottle kerosene. A full bottle cost about fifty cents in US currency and a half bottle costs about twenty-five cents. Sometimes people requested a quarter bottle as well. 'Okay,' I replied to Mama Esi and served her usual to her. Usually I would leave and come back for my payment but on that day, she mentioned that she might leave the market early and so she paid me up front. I was happy and thanked her before I went to my next customers. After serving my loyal customers—Mama Agata (pronounced: a-gar-tuh), a cassava seller, and Sister Adope (pronounced: a-doh-pe), a plantain seller—I circled around the palm oil sellers, vegetable sellers to search for new customers. As I made my way around a group of buyers surrounding the tilapia seller, I heard a request for kerosene by one of the fish sellers. Typically, a buyer would shout the name of what he or she wants and the first seller to get there would have the honor to sell to the buyer who called out.

So, when the fish seller called out that she wanted kerosene, it was a loud call for any kerosene seller in the vicinity to hear and respond to. As usual, such calls bring forth fierce competition among sellers of the same item who sprint their way to respond to the call. I looked around and made eye contact with another kerosene seller who was ready to get there before I did. He had a look of determination in his eyes. Though he was taller and older looking than me, I started to outrun him to get to the fish seller first before he did. Thanks to my agility and speed from soccer practice, I was able to cross the finish line to get to the fish seller.

Unfortunately, as I was putting my brakes on to stop myself from running over the fish seller, I slipped and fell to the ground. All my kerosene supply that was carefully measured in their respective bottles came crashing to the ground. All the bottles broke, causing the kerosene to spill everywhere. It spilled on the ground and on me as I fell to the ground with it. As you might already know, kerosene is a clear, colorless or pale yellowish color. It is somewhat odorless but when it burns, it gives off a strong smoke odor. This wasn't the first time I'd had kerosene spill on me.

Sometimes I had kerosene spill on me like when I tried to pour the kerosene into a bottle with a funnel to measure it or in some instances where I forget to seal the cap of the gallon containing the kerosene and it spilled on me. Whenever I got kerosene spill on my shirt, it took ten minutes of vigorous washing before it would come off. We didn't have baking soda or vinegar, so I would use the famous Ghanaian bar soap, key soap, to wash it repeatedly. Luckily, when I fell, the rest of the kerosene in the gallon did not spill. It was a bad day for me as a kerosene seller. At this point, the other kerosene seller who I had outpaced to get to the fish seller was laughing so loudly as if to tell me that I deserved it.

The fish seller who called out to purchase the kerosene felt bad for me and bought some of the kerosene in the gallon. She gave me some extra tip of about fifty cents to cover the broken bottles. I was in tears of course, but not about the pain I felt on my shins. I felt bad because of the disappointment of not generating enough money to support my grandparents. I cried the whole way home. My grandparents lovingly consoled me when they saw me without my kerosene bottles. They told me not to worry and expressed their love for me.

'It's okay Fifi. We appreciate everything you do to support us financially,' my grandmother consoled me.

The second time was when I had to take refuge from the storm in a little kiosk with a total stranger. I was nine years old at the time. Typically, I would leave the house around 3 pm with my gallon of kerosene, my cola bottle, and funnel, all arranged in a sack. I would walk or jog with some friends from Abossey Okai to Rot Weiss for practice from 4 pm-6 pm. Then after practice, I would take the kerosene to sell at the Kaneshie Marketplace, which is about two miles away from Rot Weiss. By the time I got home, I was exhausted. I would take a shower, eat dinner with my family, do my homework, and then sleep. I would repeat the same cycle six days a week. On good market days when I sold all my kerosene, I usually got home around 8.30 pm. However, when the market was slow, and I knew we didn't have any money at home for dinner or I had to sell all the kerosene that night to pay for the loan, I would stay out until 9.30 pm. Since we didn't have cell phones, my grandparents would be very worried and constantly prayed that I got home safe.

On that day, I had to take cover in a little kiosk at Kaneshie Market because it started raining heavily. I had just finished my route in the market; going to my usual customers and distributing the kerosene. I had about five solid customers who really liked me and would wait for me to get to the market after training. I think they liked me more because they knew I was trying to play soccer at the same time as selling kerosene. Typically, when I arrived at the market, I would go around serving kerosene to all my regular customers. My regular customers were fish, cassava, and plantain sellers. After I sold them the kerosene, they would tell me to do all my rounds of customers and then come for the money later. They didn't have the money to pay me right away, so I had to come back later after they made some sales. Sometimes when they didn't have money to pay me, they would tell me to come back the following day.

They would give me some fish or plantain to take home as interest. I understood them, and perhaps that is why they would wait for two hours to purchase the kerosene from me. It worked well for me because I was able to spend less time on the market than those that had to hunt for customers. One day after selling my kerosene, it started to drizzle. I got all the money from the customers and made my way through the congested market to head home. As I was halfway to our house, it started to rain heavily. The wind was getting stronger and I started to get soaked from the rain. It was pouring hard to the point where I needed to find a place to stay dry until it stopped raining. I sought refuge in a small wooden kiosk. I pleaded with the guy at the kiosk to let me in. It took only moments of pleading in the downpour, he was finally convinced and opened the door for me. The kiosk was filled with newspapers and had no light. I think I was in the kiosk with the man for about two hours until it stopped raining.

'What time is it?' I asked the man, as I was about to leave.

'It's 11:12 pm,' he replied.

I thanked him and continued my journey home. I got home around midnight. My grandparents were very worried. They almost sent my Uncle Evans to come after me. With no cell phone to reach out to me, they only relied on their prayers. They had an expression of relief on their faces when they saw my small, soaked body coming through the door. My grandmother gave me a big hug and asked me many times if I was okay.

'I'm fine, grandma,' I replied.

Selling kerosene was a great way for me to contribute to the family. As my grandfather would always say, 'There is no day off for a lazy person.' Everything was about hard work for me and doing the best I could to make it through the day with the family. I was determined to make each passing day better than the last. Every time I woke up in the morning and saw the blue sky, I was given a ray of hope of a better future. No matter how bad the situation was, I believed my life would not just be about selling kerosene. There is always hope for the future. I held on to that hope.

CHAPTER 4

Bastard

There was never a night or a problem that could defeat hope—
Bernard Williams

I grew up not knowing who my father was. At an early age, I knew I was fatherless because my mom and grandparents were open with me about that. There were no pictures of him in my mother's possession or at my grandparents' house. As a child born out of wedlock, by all odds, I was destined to inherit the poverty that plagued the whole country. I was called a bastard many times for not having a father. Many teased me that I was a wizard and that was why my father abandoned me. I saw little Ghanaian kids walking with their dads to school. I was, as usual, alone on my walk to school.

I have a vivid memory of playing with this little boy named Kwasi in elementary school. He was a kind, little boy who usually brought a soccer ball to school, but he was very quick-tempered. He was often seen crying or with a mad appearance on his face. We were playing with a small plastic ball that he brought to school. We started passing the ball back and forth to each other at first and then we decided to play one on one with the goal to see who could keep the ball the longest. Every time I dribbled the ball, he would just sweep my legs with his foot. After several failed attempts to get the ball back, he got frustrated and pushed me against the wall to get his ball back. I told him to calm down and that it was just a game.

'It's not my fault that you couldn't get the ball from me, Kwasi,' I said with a faint smile on my face. With tears slowly coming down his eyes, he yelled out 'adwaman ba', what translates to 'bastard' or 'child born out of wedlock.'

I was surprised at first when I heard that, and then he repeated those same words as if to make sure I heard them. I remember running away from the scene in tears. How did Kwasi come to that conclusion? I never told him about my family. Then it dawned on me that Kwasi came to that conclusion because I was often with my mother and grandparents at school or perhaps, he overheard my mom telling the principal that my father was not in my life.

Although my height at the time was close to my grandfather's, the resemblance gave it away. All the children could tell that I was with my grandfather instead of my dad. My grandfather became a father to me and attended all my school meetings. These words 'adwaman ba' (pronounced: eh-dwar-man-ba) or hohwini,' (pronounced: hoh-we-knee) would become the bane of my childhood, causing me to cry every time I heard them. I couldn't count how many times I cried because of those words. I thought that my tears would eventually dry up. I would often complain to my grandparents and they would look me straight in the eyes and say, 'Fifi, you're a great boy and destined for a great future. Don't let those words change who you are. We are here for you.'

Although my father was out of sight, I was surrounded by a loving family who constantly reminded me of how special I was.

'Bastard,' 'prophesied,' 'special' ... Those words became part of who I was and would help me to cling on to the hope I had. In fact, I was imbued with a strong sense of confidence in the future. Any time I heard the word 'bastard,' I would remember 'prophesied' and 'special.' Those words became my source of motivation, to work hard and make sure I became the best person my grandparents saw in me. I have often wondered what life could've been for me if my father hadn't abandoned me. Maybe I would have been groomed by my father to become a soldier, just like him. Maybe I would be working in a factory in Ghana. Whatever my life may have been, I'm thankful for where I am and the person that I've become now. I truly do believe that everything happens for a reason.

As strange as it may seem, I think that the desire to take control of my life comes directly from my personality and the fact that I was abandoned by my father. It made me independent and certainly hardworking.

I think I developed the attitude of working hard, so I could do well and make my father wish he didn't abandon me. Thanks to the loving support of my grandparents, my mom, my uncles and aunt, I never felt abandoned. I felt special, and particularly optimistic about becoming successful in the future. My optimistic nature was tested on many occasions.

On one occasion when I was sickened by hunger, I almost ran away from my grandparents to look for my father. The last location I had in mind for him was Burma Camp. Although very far from where my grandparents lived, I was determined to walk and hitchhike to look for him. However, I couldn't bear the sight of disappointing my grandparents with this audacious move. Every time that idea popped into my head, I would just drop it at the sight of my grandparents. They made me feel as though my father never existed. On another occasion, when I was suspended from school for not being able to pay for my school fees, I thought about stealing.

In fact, stealing was very common at the time but highly frowned upon. In Ghana when people are caught stealing, a mob of vigilantes will appear from nowhere and enforce their own sense of justice by mercilessly beating the thief to death or cutting one or two of their fingers off to remind them of their bad deed. I was spared a life of crime because of my ineptitude at thievery. One day I saw a mob attack a man for stealing a chicken at someone's back yard. The mob severely beat him and would have almost killed him if the owner of the chicken hadn't pitied him and begged the mob to let him go.

I was so terrified that I vowed to never steal in my life. I was surrounded with love despite the chaos of poverty and that was enough to spare me a life of crime. With hope, I embraced my past and worked hard in the present to create a better future for me and my family. Although afraid and fatherless, I spent my childhood years under the loving care of my grandparents. In Ghana, it was uncommon for children to live with their grandparents due to economic hardship. My grandparents broke their backs every day in the blazing heat of Ghana to provide any meal on the table and to put a roof over our heads.

Sometimes we were fortunate to get two meals a day and we would drink lots of water to feel full. I spent a lot of time with my grandfather in the absence of my father. My grandfather was a short, bald man with a big heart for God. He spent most of his time teaching us about God and continued to remind us to never lose faith and stay focused on our hope of a better future. Filled with great life experience, my grandfather used to tell us stories about life, and how our actions can influence our future. Whether his stories were real or fictional, they always seemed to carry a deeper, inspiring meaning.

I loved his stories; especially the one where the woman fell in love with a ghost after refusing marriage proposals from men from her village. The story goes like this:

There was a beautiful girl by the name Adjoa, in the village of Ukeri. Everyone in the village was mesmerized by her beauty and often complimented her as she walked by. In fact, she was the most beautiful girl in the whole village. As a result of this beauty, the woman became very arrogant and very rude. She rejected every marriage proposal from the men in and outside the village. She even rejected the chief's son, Ekute's proposal to be the next in line as queen of the village. She would yell at those men who dared to ask her for marriage.

'Good for nothing men. Ugly men with no future ahead of you. I want a man with money. A handsome man who can take care of me,' she would say to them as they shamefully walked away with their bride price in hand.

Her parents advised her to look beyond looks and money and look for a good man in her choice of mate, but they often met their suggestions with all the insults of the world. Then one day a stranger from a different village came to visit the village. He was tall and handsome and appeared to be very rich because he was dazzled in gold. As soon as Adjoa saw the way the man was dressed, she was immediately attracted to his wealth. Nobody in the village knew where the man came from and was very cautious about him.

They warned the woman to make a thorough investigation about the man before being drawn to him, but she disrespectfully refused their advice. He proposed to Adjoa, and despite failed attempts by her parents to convince her to reject the proposal, Adjoa accepted it without thinking twice. They immediately got married and left the village to their own home. The woman was gone for many years and nobody knew where they went. Her parents became very worried and sent people to search for them.

The searchers went around visiting many of the neighboring villages asking for their whereabouts, but nobody has heard of the man or his family before. Everybody became very worried and news began to spread that the woman had been kidnaped or died. Many years passed and still, nothing was heard about the woman. Until one day, a very old looking woman appeared in the village of Ukeri with a flesh-eating disease spread all over her body.

Nobody recognized her, and many started pointing fingers at her. She eventually stumbled up to the chief's palace and told them that her name is Adjoa, the beautiful woman that went away with the man. Nobody believed her at first because she looked old—even older than her parents. She began to mention her parents' names and revealed information about her family that proved that she was indeed, Adjoa.

The chief immediately gathered the whole village and they asked why she had returned. Most of the villagers kept pointing fingers and asking each other, if this was truly Adjoa? What really happened to her? Adjoa tearfully explained that the man was a ghost and she lived with him at the cemetery far away from home. She got old because she had to clean the cemetery every day and she became a slave for the man for all these years. Finally, she was set free by the man and made her way to find her village.

My grandfather's stories ended abruptly. This was among the many fun and educational stories that my grandfather told us when I was young. I always looked forward to his stories. I had a firm belief in education too. My future goal was to become a meteorologist. I wanted to know why Ghana was so hot and had no snow. My meteorological dream slowly began to evaporate as I became fully involved with playing soccer, selling kerosene, and helping my Uncle Evans with his carpentry job. Meanwhile, my mother remarried, Bro Oko, a bookkeeper at the Kaneshie market and they moved to Abeka, a two-hour drive from Abossey Okai due to the daunting traffic. My mom left with my other siblings, but I stayed with my grandparents to continue my study, play soccer, and support my grandparents with kerosene. Almost in a similar fashion, my aunt Juliet also remarried Bro Oweredu, (pronounced: oh-we-red-u) and they stayed together at my grandparents rented apartment. They stayed with us a few months until they moved to Kasoa, a three-hour drive from Abossey Okai. With my mom and Aunt Juliet out of the apartment, it came down to my grandparents, my Uncles Evans and Emma, myself, and my two cousins. There were now seven of us at the apartment, following the same routine of struggling to survive each passing day.

CHAPTER 5

Rot Weiss: The journey begins

Where there is no hope in the future, there is no power in the present—
John Maxwell

I have loved soccer ever since I was a young child when I would ride on my mother's back carrying a small plastic ball in my hand. I started playing soccer barefoot with my Uncle Emma and some friends in any open dirt space in our neighborhood. It felt very natural playing barefoot but sometimes you get cuts from loose rocks or broken bottles hidden under the sand.

I didn't have to look too far for inspiration to play soccer growing up. When you turn every street corner of Ghana, you will see children playing soccer, whether at school or in the neighborhoods. Every space—whether sand or gravel—is engulfed by young children hoping to achieve a better life through soccer. My grandfather was my biggest inspiration. He used to tell us that he played a lot of soccer in the village of Ajumako.

He was very good and had the finest skills in soccer. It was very hard to believe him at first, considering his five-foot frame, but his love for soccer proved otherwise. Unfortunately, he didn't get the opportunity to use his soccer to escape poverty. He loved the sport so much that he would sneak behind people's windows listening to any soccer game being broadcast on the radio. He was a die-hard supporter of the Abusua Dwarfs (pronounced: eh-boo-su-ah), a local team from the Ghanaian Premier League. I used to think that the Abusua Dwarfs were a team filled with dwarfs or short people, and I thought my grandfather loved the Abusua Dwarfs because of his height.

It turned out that was not the case—the Abusua Dwarfs came from the central region of Ghana, the birthplace of my grandfather's hometown, Ajumako. My grandfather always checked the sports section of the local newspaper, looking for game scores or any news about the Abusua Dwarfs. He would argue for a very long time with the neighbors over individual players he felt should be called into the Ghanaian national team—most of these players from the Abusua Dwarfs, of course.

During World Cup season, he would often watch his black and white television that he received as a bonus through his work. He loved listening to sports commentary and would often force me to listen to the commentary with him, as he cheered happily to every goal scored by the Abusua Dwarfs.

I spent as much time as possible outside playing soccer on the graveled space near our house. From a very young age, I spent almost every minute I could playing soccer at school or at home, usually with my friends or my Uncle Emma. We sometimes played right in the compound underneath all the clothing lines with a plastic soccer ball that we made from plastic bags and pieces of paper.

I started turning the heads of the people in our neighborhood with my soccer skills when I was about seven years old. At this point, I had countless hours of street soccer experience under my belt and gained the experience of playing against older boys. I had also experienced the pain of getting kicked in soccer, especially when I received those two-footed 'African tackles,' and they complained they got 'all ball' when clearly, they got 'all of my ankles.' I also experienced the tiredness that came along with chasing people to get a touch of the tired, plastic-rubber ball that was covered in mud.

My fate to join a more organized soccer team finally came when I got the opportunity to join my Uncle Emma's team, Rot-Weiss. One day after a bad game, Emma's coach became very angry and uttered some harsh words about their poor performance. In the heat of that moment, the coach looked over to where I was standing and asked whose brother I was. Emma answered quickly, 'He's my brother.'

Immediately the coach said, 'I'm sure this little boy could've played better in the game than all of you.'

Afterward, he instructed Emma to bring me to practice the next day, and from there, my soccer journey began. It was Monday and I had just returned home from my afternoon school session. My Uncle Emma was waiting to take me to practice as the coach insisted. I was very excited and quickly put on the worn-out running shoes Emma passed on to me. We arrived at practice and the coach gave me a warm welcome. That week was full of learning for me. I was used to playing on the streets or on our school playground but never on a big sandy field. I looked to run all over the place, but my technique and several passes proved my understanding of the game. I was moved to play right back for the team. Emma was already the 'general' midfielder for the team. He was arguably the best player on the team who was spraying passes in all directions. My first game for Emma's team was against Cosmos FC. The game was played on a big gravel field, causing players to skate by when they are running at top speed and their opponent abruptly stops the ball. I was on the bench at the start of the game and was the smallest player on both teams. I was playing against an U10 team and I was about seven at the time.

The coach thought very hard about whether to play me or not, fearing that I might get injured in such a physical game on the worst field you could possibly imagine. During halftime, he looked at me several times and he finally gave in to my impatient desire to play. It was ten minutes left in the game and he instructed me to substitute in for the right back position. At this point, we were winning two-nil. I was very happy as I sprinted on the field with my baggy soccer jersey dangling around my tiny body.

Right-back was full of running as I spent most of my time running with my opponent to prevent them from scoring. I completed a few passes down the line for our right midfielder and received a couple of passes from Emma. After the game, they all congratulated me for hanging in there with the big boys. I went to Emma and tucked on his shirt.

'Emma, Emma...,' he looked down at me with a smile. 'I'm so tired,' I told him.

Emma burst into laughter and immediately told the whole team who tease me for those comments to this day. I was indeed very tired for the ten minutes I played and because of the way I was teased, I vowed in my heart that I would never show that vulnerability again in my life.

I started to run every day after school. Did I mention that Rot-Weiss was forty-five minutes away from where I lived? I would run forty-five minutes every day after school to go to practice with Emma and some friends. The crowded, smoky street from Abossey Okai (pronounced: ah-bos-say oh-ka-e) to Awudome (a-wu-doh-mey) was full of stalls. Food vendors and traders hawked a multitude of goods from children selling ice water to women carrying plastic buckets, mangoes, fried plantain, and plastic laundry basket with their babies on their backs.

The air smelled like grilled fish mixed with emissions from rusted exhaust pipes from the moving cars. From the cries of babies on their mother's backs to cars honking and food vendors calling out for customers, the road sounded very loud but a good distraction for long distance running. After a series of runs to Rot-Weiss, I began to condition my lungs and my body to keep up with the speed of play. My hard work paid off one day at practice. That day was fitness day. No soccer, just running and agility work. We started going around the field and one lap slowly grew into ten and fifteen and twenty laps. A lot of the older players were walking by now, except for just a few of us. That day I discovered how much oxygen my lungs could retain. I had endurance to run for days; endurance to face life's struggles with perseverance.

After a few months of playing with Emma's U10 team, Bro Atta created an U8 team that was built around me. I was made the captain of the team and was moved from the right-back position to central midfielder. I took all our set pieces including corner kicks and free kicks for the team because of my technique. I scored a lot of free kicks for Rot-Weiss and had many assists from my corners. One of my most fond and proudest moments of playing at Rot-Weiss was when I scored the game-winning goal against Bees United FC. It was an evenly matched game with a bundle of chances from both sides until we broke the deadlock at the beginning of the second half.

It was a corner kick I took which was met with Kojo's head—a smallish center back we had at the time—and the ball found its way to the back of the net. Bees United FC proved stubborn and responded with a series of attacks. Their coach sent a lot of his players forward to get the equalizer, turning the game into onslaughts of counterattacks. Ten minutes until the final whistle, Bees United FC got their equalizer through an own goal from a deflection. At this point, the game was headlining to a tie and the whole field was filled with wild anticipation.

Both coaches were on their feet as the clock wound down to the last few minutes. We got a free kick and we sent everyone into the opponents' box except for our goalie. I sent a long ball into the box and they cleared it. As it bounced several times over a couple of players, it made its way to be middle of the field, towards my direction.

Without thinking of receiving it first, I shot it first time towards their goal and saw the ball go over their goalkeeper and into the top right corner. The whole field went wild. Emma's team who were supporting on the sideline came rushing to the field. Our coach, Bro Atta, sprinted towards my direction and lifted me up, like a king whose feet were not allowed to touch the ground.

It was the first and only time Bro Atta had ever lifted a player after a win. It was a special moment for me and one of the proudest moments of my soccer career. From the moment on, soccer became my life.

Soccer was my only escape from life's anxiety. I would play soccer at home, at school, and at Rot-Weiss. In fact, Rot-Weiss became my second home. I always longed to go and practice. I would sometimes go there on our off days with some friends to kick around or walk on the dirt field envisioning myself scoring goals and playing on TV someday. Most of the time, Emma and I would bring our kerosene with us to sell on the way to practice, and then would sell the rest of the kerosene at Kaneshie Market, on our way back from practice. My love for the sport took away the dread of walking to practice every day.

My whole life was centered on playing soccer and helping my grandparents. I arrived at training one day and our coach, Bro Atta, called us all together.

He said, 'We are going to have a white coach for the next two weeks. I will be here to facilitate him but make sure you pay attention to him. His name is Andrew Farrant and he will be here tomorrow to train with the team. There is a new soccer academy in Ghana, and we will be playing a tournament on the weekends and the best players will have the opportunity to be selected.'

Everyone was ecstatic hearing the words tournament, scouting, and especially a white coach. In Africa, anything associated with white people or as the locals call them, 'obroni' is associated with good. Any obroni walking down the street of Africa is assumed to be wealthy and ushered with respect and praise. Sadly, when I'm walking down the street with an obroni and we both need help, many Africans will gravitate to helping the obroni instead of one of their own people.

It is very interesting because even though there is a history of slavery and the taking away of many of Africa's resources by Europeans, we still see all whites as saviors and offer them the best treatment.

We were very happy to start training with Andy, the new white coach, and hopefully, we would get selected. This was our gateway to escape the chaotic shadows of poverty in pursuit of successes. We'd been training on this dead patch of half gravel, half sand field for too long and it was about time we made a change. As we were leaving with that news, Bro Atta called me back. I was still the captain for the U10 team at the time.

He said, 'Fifi, you're definitely the best player of this group. Everyone here knows that. I want you to bring your best soccer to training throughout these two weeks and I believe you will make it.' Those words sent a sharp burst of nerves through my body.

I was nervous and yet excited for this big opportunity. This could finally be my moment! 'Thanks, Coach, I will do my best. God is on my side,' I replied nervously. I went and picked up my kerosene bag and left.

I usually went back to the market to sell my kerosene after practice but on this special day, I decided to go straight home. My walk back home was filled with mixed feelings. I didn't know what to think or how I should act. I was so excited that by the time I realized I was home, I told my family about this news and they were very happy for the opportunity. I washed my best worn-out soccer jersey and shorts that my Uncle Emma, had bought for me years ago.

I also cleaned out the dirt on my torn-out Togo-made cleats. The term 'Togo-made' is what we refer to as fake and cheap clothes or shoes found in the Ghanaian market. I spent most of the night making sure every piece of dirt was off my shoes. I prayed to God that if He ever were to bless me in my soccer playing, to give it to me for the next two weeks. I was confident that if I could do my best, God would be there for me and I would be selected.

The next day at practice, I was the first to arrive. Shortly after I got there, more and more players started showing up. The news that a white coach coming to Rot-Weiss brought many children who were not even on the team to play soccer. I was surprised to see that Rot-Weiss had so many U10 players. There were about thirty kids there which was three times more than the usual number of players that would show up to practice every day. Andy Farrant showed up in his clean England national team red shirt and White shorts with white socks. We were all ecstatic and could barely understand him as he welcomed us and explained his reasons why he was to be our coach for the next two weeks.

Most of us could hardly understand what Andrew was saying, but we all nodded our heads in agreement to whatever he was saying. With little or no education, most of us grew up speaking Ga (g-ah), Twi (t-wee), Fante (f-ahn-the) or Hausa (ha-u-sah). These are a few examples of the Ghanaian languages or dialects. Ghana is divided into ten regions, and each reaching has its main language or dialect. Ga is mostly spoken by people from the Greater Accra region of Ghana. Twi is commonly spoken by people from Ashanti Region. Fante is spoken in the central region of Ghana and Hausa is spoken by people from the northern region of Ghana. Although we all couldn't understand English, we all spoke the same language of soccer.

I have always been passionate about my education as much as soccer. The Universal Declaration of Human Rights makes it clear that every child has the right to a free, basic education so that poverty and lack of money should not be a barrier to schooling. Because of this, over the last decade, in many developing countries like Ghana, governments have announced the abolition of school fees and as a result, there have been impressive increases in the number of children going to school. However, for many of the poorest families in Ghana, education remains too expensive and the children are forced to stay at home doing chores or selling things to support their families.

Unfortunately, families remain locked in a cycle of poverty that goes on for generations. In many countries in Africa, while education is theoretically free, in practice 'informal fees' see parents forced to pay for 'compulsory items' like uniforms, books, pens, extra lessons, exam fees or funds to support the school buildings. In other places, the lack of functioning public government schools means that parents have no choice but to send their children to private schools that, even if they are 'low fee,' are unaffordable for the poorest families who risk making themselves destitute in their efforts to get their children better lives through education. Soccer was the only viable option for most poor, young children in Ghana. Soccer not only kept us in shape, but it also distracted us from the poverty that surrounded us and gave us this sense of hope to a better future.

Most Ghanaian kids had a lot more interest in the school's dirt soccer field than its classroom. The dirt field is the most popular place in the school. The field is usually filled with kids during breaks and after school.

Women set up wooden tables selling local Ghanaian food like rice, kenkey (kane-kay), fish, banku (ban-kuh), drinks, and grilled plantain. There are usually teams of kids playing on the field and the kids who weren't playing with shagged balls in their brown and yellow school uniforms. Whereas most kids had little interest or gave up on school altogether, I was always one of the kids who would play but still paid attention to my studies.

I remember one day we were playing barefoot outside our classroom on the playground during class time. We used the remains of cement blocks to make goal posts. The teacher was late to class, so some of my classmates persuaded me into going outside to play. We bolted from our wooden desks and went out to play our favorite game, 'four corners.' The term 'four corners' came from the four directions of the world, the cardinal points—north, south, east, and west commonly denoted by their initials N, E, S, and W. We used half-bricks or abandoned blocks or a stack of stones to make goals at each of the corners and each goal is about five yards from each other.

Each person starts by standing in the middle of their randomly assigned goal and there is only one touch or kick per person. One player starts with the plastic ball that we use, and the objective of the game is to get a player out of the goal when it's their time to kick or to score and then quickly score on them before they get back to their goal. Once you get scored on, you are eliminated and the three will play until we get one winner. When you are in the middle, it looked like you were standing at an intersection where you can go forward, right, left, or backward.

This is a very strategic game which required a lot of thinking, passing, and shooting. It gets intense and they start shooting the ball hard at you to get you out of your goal. After a few minutes of playing 'four corners,' our teacher comes storming out to the playground and ushers us into the classroom. As we were running to get to class, she stopped me in my tracks and said,

'I'm disappointed in you, Kingsley Baiden.' In Ghana, whenever a teacher uses your full name to address you, it is a sign of something very good or bad, and in this situation, my fate was with the latter.

This was when I realized that she was very disappointed. 'You are a very bright student and you are letting these boys bring you down with them,' she added. I listened with my head down to avoid eye contact and left after she was done talking.

Unlike the Western culture, which requires eye contact with the person you are talking to, African culture sees eye contact, especially with an elderly person as a sign of disrespect. We are to listen silently without talking back and making eye contact and if you dare to do the opposite, then you will be in a big trouble. As my teacher was talking, I kept wondering why she was only talking to me?

My three other classmates were already in the class. I cried, knowing that I let my teacher down, but I still didn't get why she only spoke to me and didn't have a word with my other classmates who I was playing with on the playground. Why was she attacking me? Why were my classmates not attacked? These were the thoughts that went through my head throughout the rest of the day. It took me a whole day, but I came to the realization that she cared about me and believed in my future.

Growing up, I didn't have my mom or dad reading bedtime stories to me or anybody taking the time to help me with my reading. I started learning English by reading signposts as I walked the streets. I would ask people, what does the sign say on the store front? What does this mean? What is this? How do you pronounce this word or that word? My curiosity and desire to learn English helped me to pick up a lot of words in English quicker than children at my age at the time.

I was able to use the little English I knew then to help my teammates to heed Andrew's instructions on the field. It didn't take long for Andrew to be dazzled by my soccer skills. We were working on a passing drill and he often praised my passing technique and my understanding of the game. This is a great sign of a good day, I thought to myself.

After the session, Andrew told me to 'keep it up and continue to work hard.' I was beaming with confidence since the first day, and I quickly formulated a friendship with Andrew after that. We cracked jokes here and there, and he would often advise me on the areas of my game that I needed to improve on to make it to the next level.

Our first game of the tournament was hosted at our home field at Rot-Weiss. It was a very difficult place to play for the opposing team because of its sandiness and slope. The sand at Rot-Weiss felt like playing at the beach. Most opponents got tired after the first half of the game and then they would take the beating in the second half. We won our first game of the tournament, a four-one thumping over Mandela FC. I scored a free kick fifteen minutes into the game and had one assist. Our tall, lanky forward, Samuel Boateng, popularly known as 'Kay,' scored a hat-trick that day. He was a technical forward with an eye for the goal. He was bursting with confidence leading into the tournament. Andrew was very happy with the team performance and congratulated us for our effort.

All my teammates were overjoyed and couldn't wait for the next game. We were away for our next game against the Future Stars. It was a hard-fought game, with the Future Stars coming off from a loss of their first game. The game became a tug of war with both teams putting pressure on attack. I was playing my usual position as a central midfielder. I was connecting most of my passes and winning tackles in the middle of the field. Kay was making some good runs, but the graveled field made the game hard to establish a flow. There were a lot of bounces of the ball and it was affecting our final passes in the opponent's half. Shot after shot sailed over the crossbar, leading to a stalemate at the end of the game. We now had four points and were on top of our group.

As we progressed to the quarter finals, we faced Dezac's Sporting Club, a team with a lot of really good players. They topped their group, winning all their games and coming into the game with a lot of confidence. The game was played at Kwashieman (K-wah-she-ma), a small town in Accra. The game was played on a small, and overly-used field that was outlined with old car tires half immersed into the ground. The sunken tires provide a nice sitting spot for the spectators who also had the choice of standing on concrete terraces that ran down the field.

The field was lined with little pieces of charcoal to demarcate the boundaries of the field. The home team players usually spent hours and hours marking the field with a long rope and charcoal pieces. Unlike Rot-Weiss, which was located next to Awudome Middle school, Dezac's field was located across a busy road of crowded sellers of both young children and adults. Andy called me aside before this game and told me he'd been really impressed with the way I'd been playing at practice and in the games and that I had made it as one of the players scouted by the Rigt to Dream Academy.

I was very happy to hear the news, yet I wondered why he called me to tell me that right before our most crucial game of the tournament? Perhaps he wanted to motivate me to rally the team, and his plan worked. Within the first five minutes, Dezac's scored from a missed controlled back pass by Boga, who was a strong and fearless kid with the ability to shoulder off his opponent with his size. The goal opened the game as both teams were technical enough to possess the ball. That was my best game of the whole tournament.

I was playing with so much confidence and moving the ball as fast as possible as if I was playing a musical instrument. I was connecting one to two passes in the middle of the field like a spider building its web. We came back from our first goal deficit from a long pass from a long-distance goal. I scored from a lay off from Kay. It all progressed from a long pass from our left back towards Kay. As a good reader of the game, I saw their goalkeeper off from his line and as Kay was controlling the ball in the air, I yelled 'set.' Set is a term we used a lot in Ghana to demand a first-time lay off from your teammate to put the ball at a good position for you to strike it first time.

Hearing my loud voice, Kay immediately laid the ball off with his chest and I struck the ball first time catching everyone including the goalkeeper by surprise until the ball hit the back of the net—it was game on! My teammates rushed to hug me, and Kay started making gestures with his hand towards his head, signaling an intelligent play on my part. I looked over and saw Andrew with his thumbs up as he caught my eyes. The game went into half-time with both teams having the confidence of winning the game.

The second half was a great game—aggressive, intense, fun and a full showcase of talent. We gave up a last-minute goal from a corner kick as we failed to clear the ball from our box. It was a hard blow to the team, but a performance that kept our heads high. Fans from both teams were very entertained, clapping with big smiles as we walked off the dirt field, marked with small pieces of charcoal. Our jerseys were covered in sweat, dirt and black spots from the charcoal. Andrew gave us all high-fives and expressed his utmost pleasure to be our coach.

He also told us that Right to Dream would contact us individually about the selection. We went home with our hearts filled with excitement and hope of being selected by Right to Dream. Not surprisingly, Dezac's went on to win the whole tournament. A week went by with no news from Andy and from Right to Dream. As the days went by, many of my teammates became impatient, constantly asking our main coach, Bro Atta, if he had heard any news. I, on the other hand, remained calm and continued to train even harder. I had an upper hand because Andrew had already told me that I would be selected, and my performance from the tournament, especially the last game, hit the nail on the head.

Despite this confidence, I continued to show up to every practice and worked on my own to improve on the areas of the game that Andy suggested I focus on. Every Sunday, I would jog over five miles from Abbossey Okay to Korle Gonno Beach (pronounced: K-or-lay Gone-oh) or popularly referred to as 'Dogo' (pronounced: Dough-go) with my friend and teammate, Seth Biney. Dogo is one of Ghana's most popular beaches but it's not a good view for tourists. The beach is usually dirty with a lot of plastic waste but the stench that emanates from the beach does not keep away desperate young Ghanaian athletes from jogging to workout at the beach every weekend. Seth Biney and I would do some sprints and agility work at the beach. Back at my house, I would also gather a couple of little kids in the neighborhood to play barefoot with them, dribbling through them as they tried very hard to win the ball back with their short, little legs.

We got to practice on Monday, and Bro Atta had a meeting with us. He mentioned that Andy and Right to Dream came by his house and expressed interest in selecting two of us for a final tryout in Dawu (pronounced: d-ay-woo) in the eastern part of Ghana.

'The two names are...' as soon he said that the whole place went quiet and you could see our chests rising as we nervously wait for our turn. You could feel the anxiety, the nervousness, and the attentiveness of each one of us as we awaited our fate. Bro Atta cleared his throat and continued, 'the two players that Right to Dream are interested in are Fifi and Kay.'

The mentioning of my name didn't come as a surprise to me or my teammates, but it was a relief. Some of my teammates started to cry and we tried to console them. Bro Atta wished Kay and me the best of luck and encouraged the rest of my teammates not to give up hope.

'God works in mysterious ways boys,' he said, 'keep your head up and keep working hard. Don't lose hope, your time will come.' Kay and

I were very happy, but we knew that the work was not done. The real work lay ahead of us and we needed to focus to compete with other players selected from all over Ghana. We had a week to prepare and get ready to meet for the final tryout in Dawu.

As I hurried home that evening, filled with excitement to break the news to my family, I stopped by Kaneshie market, about six miles from Rot-Weiss to finish selling the kerosene I had left. I spent an hour in the market and sold all the kerosene before heading home. Knowing there was no money at home for dinner, I bought a few groceries with part of the profit to take to my family. As soon as I got home, my grandmother was very excited about the groceries and expressed how happy she was that I sold all the kerosene.

I handed the groceries to my grandmother and told her I had some good news. Before I could tell her, my nieces and cousins, my Uncle Evans, coming from his work as a carpenter, also walked into the room. I told them the news that I had been invited by Right to Dream for a month-long final tryout in Dawu and had to report there in a week. They were overjoyed by the news and started praising God and dancing in the room. Being part of a soccer academy is a big deal in Ghana because it meant that all the burden of the basic needs of life—food, clothing, shelter, and education—will be removed from the family by the academies.

Also, when a player makes it to the professional level, then it will mean that there is more money to take care of the family. News about my selection spread through the neighborhood, as I got a lot of hugs and congratulations from passing friends and neighbors.

The week leading up to embarking to Dawu was filled with excitement, nervousness, and hope. First, I didn't know what to take along for what could be a month-long tryout and I didn't know whether to pack light or more to last for the whole month. Filled with confidence and hope, my heart chose the latter. I didn't have a lot of clothes at the time, so I only packed the few soccer clothes and worn-out 'Togo-made' soccer shoes that I owned, putting them in the brand-new black plastic bag that I bought after selling kerosene. We didn't have enough money for my trip, so I sold kerosene the whole week to save up some money for my transportation to Dawu. This was the first time I would be leaving my home in Accra to a different part of Ghana.

Either way, I was very thankful for the opportunity and looked forward to making the best out of it. I went through a series of rigorous training sessions with Seth and Kay, running back and forth to Dogo Beach every day and working on our passing and shooting techniques.

My family had always been very supportive of my soccer endeavors through prayer and allowing me to go to training and playing games instead of mainly focusing on my education and selling kerosene. That week leading up to leaving to Dawu was more of a prayer week for my family. As the days went by, they increased the length of their prayer and how often they prayed. My grandmother was full of confidence that I would make it because she believed she prayed hard enough that week.

'Fifi, God has answered our prayers. You just have to believe and do your best,' she constantly reminded me each day.

The day finally came for me to leave. I said my final goodbyes to my family and close friends, and my Uncle Evans decided to accompany me to Dawu since it was my first time travelling out of Accra. He told me that he would leave as soon as he dropped me off. We walked from Abossey Okai to Kaneshie to get transportation from there to Dawu.

CHAPTER 6

Right to Dream Academy

The future belongs to those who believe in the beauty of their dreams –
Eleanor Roosevelt

Every child has the right to dream[i]. This inalienable right of becoming whatever we want to become in the future is just a mere dream for most Ghanaian children living in extreme poverty. Growing up as a child, I dreamt of becoming a meteorologist. I wanted to learn about the weather. It didn't take me too long to do away with that dream after I quickly realized that my family was just working from hand to mouth.

My family had no money to pay for my education, and all the income generated went straight into feeding us. Sadly, instead of having big dreams, many children walked around the dusty roads of Ghana begging and hustling for food. Ghana's history with poverty is inexcusable for a country that was formerly known as 'The Gold Coast.'

At this point, I want you to close your eyes and picture yourself time travelling to the year of 1957. It was the year Ghana gained its independence from our British colonizers and became the first sub-Saharan nation to break free from colonial rule. The country was in great jubilation. There was music and dancing, and many Ghanaian children dressed in their flamboyant and colorful Ghanaian dresses. The Ghanaian flag was waving as the wind blew.

At this point, you made your way through the dancing crowd to stand in the front row of the platform, next to the dancing mothers. Without understanding any of the lyrics to the songs, you started to sway from side to side. You were dancing excitedly for the great celebration. Dr Kwame Nkrumah, Ghana's first Prime Minister, stepped up the podium to address the jubilant crowd on this memorable day. The music stopped and you stood attentively to hear every word of his message.

'Ghana,' Nkrumah began, moving the crowd to loud cheering and clapping. You started clapping as well with the crowd.

After a few moments of cheering, the crowd was silenced again as Nkrumah continued with his speech.

'Ghana, our beloved country, is free forever,' Nkrumah said those words with so much hope and potential that sent the whole crowd into a wild cheer. You were in tears of joy hearing that the people of Ghana are free, not just in the moment, but forever. Despite the music and dancing, you paused, and began to wonder what that freedom meant.

Now, I want you to open your eyes and picture the state of Ghana today. What do you think of when you hear of Ghana or Africa in general? Your first thought was perhaps poverty, diseases, or the vibrant African culture. This harsh reality of the state of Ghana is a far cry from the freedom that our first prime minister, Dr Kwame Nkrumah, proclaimed with such great conviction. Poverty has stripped off every right of the Ghanaian people, forcing many Ghanaians like my grandparents to give up on the freedom that Dr Kwame Nkrumah 'promised.'

This right to dream big and become doctors and lawyers and engineers is farfetched for many Ghanaian children. Soccer is the vehicle of hope from poverty. Many Ghanaian children play soccer every day to pass time and to improve on their soccer skills. This pool of young talented soccer players could be exploited. This is where Right to Dream stepped in with the vision of restoring the rights of every talented soccer player in Ghana to have a dream and dream big. I was one of those young boys whose right to dream was restored.

The story of Right to Dream is far more interesting than just another 'white savior' coming to Africa to bring about change to benefit themselves, whether through force or persuasion. It is about a young, ambitious man by the name Tom Vernon who came all the way from Britain to Ghana to make the most out of the resources available in Ghana. Although Africa has many resources like gold, diamonds, and oil, its biggest resource is the pool of talented young soccer players desperately looking for an opportunity for a better life. In 1999, Tom Vernon recognized that need and founded the Right to Dream Academy to provide an opportunity to young talented Ghanaian soccer players. Right to Dream Academy started from humble beginnings in Teshie, a suburb of Accra, the capital of Ghana.

I visited the Teshie residence and it was very small compared to what the Right to Dream facilities are now. Tom and his team including

Samuel Mawuena, Benjamin Adjei, and Gareth Henderby tried out over eighty children and offered full scholarships to only fifteen of them. These fifteen players became what we call in Ghana the 'the First Generation.' Over time, Right to Dream expanded from the First Generation to a second, third, and fourth generation of boys. Then, the vision shifted to include girls. This inclusion of a girls' program was monumental for the academy because of the perceived gender roles in Africa. In Ghana and Africa in general, traditional gender roles have shaped the way boys and girls are perceived in all aspects of society.

In Ghana, girls were discouraged from engaging in contact sports such as soccer. Playing soccer was seen as unfeminine. Any girl that tried to play soccer was considered a 'lesbian' or 'man-woman' as the locals called it. Being a 'man-woman' was highly frowned upon in Ghana and led to the ostracizing of many girls.

Most girls became comfortable to be confined at home and didn't dare to try playing soccer as they were afraid to be labelled as a 'man-woman.' As a result, by establishing the girls' program, Right to Dream gave talented young girls from across West Africa the chance to break social norms, build their confidence, gain a top education, and become future leaders.

Right to Dream Academy has the mission to get the best talent from every part of Ghana. That's a daunting task that requires lots of travel time for scouting and lots of money. In order to do this, Right to Dream put together soccer tournaments among all the colt teams (or youth teams) from all over Ghana to pick out the best talent. Using volunteers as head coaches for the respective colt teams, they are able to scout the best talents in all these colt teams.

It was a difficult spot for Right to Dream though to analyse all of us and get the best talent possible. There were a lot of good players at the tryouts and it was difficult to let most of us go. I wondered since nobody can foretell the future, how could they determine whether the ten players that will be chosen are really the cream of the top?

There were many kids who started exceptionally good at a young age but lacked consistency and as they grew older, they slowly declined in performance. This might be the result of many factors on and off the field that affected their progress. The biggest stumbling block in a player's performance is injury. Sometimes a player can be out with injury for a while, ranging from six weeks to a whole year depending on the severity of the injury. It takes a lot of hard work and a strong mental capacity to get back to playing at a high level after injury.

Like all athletes, I've had my fair share of injuries, from ankle sprains, a head injury requiring stitches and a hip surgery which put me out of soccer for a whole year. When you are injured, your fitness level drops, you lose your muscle mass, you become 'rusty' in your technical ability, and you also lose your confidence. Another factor that affects a player's performance is personal problems in their life. One personal problem might be struggling with grades at school, forcing them to spend more time studying and less time improving their soccer skills. Another problem might be family breakdown such as divorce that can affect a child's motivation to work hard.

One very significant problem though that most African athletes face is pressure from family members. When these children make it to the top, they often get burned out from family pressure for financial assistance. They feel an intense responsibility to help their people back home and wire significant amounts of money back home. The perception in Africa is that once you make it to the top, you're automatically rich.

Your family members and friends ask for financial assistance constantly. Most Africans lose the joy of playing soccer because of the financial pressures. Another problem is that most kids lose their focus to work hard, to maintain their potential at the top. I have seen a lot of great players fall off their path especially in youth soccer where they start off being too good for their age group and eventually fade away. Unlike these children, there are other children who start off very slowly but never give up and keep working hard until they became the best. Tim Nokte wrote this famous quote which was brought to light by NBA superstar Kevin Durant when he was being drafted to the NBA in 2007: 'Hard work beats talent unless talent works hard.' Most talented children fall off the radar because of their inability to train at the highest level to continue to improve to be the best.

Luckily for Right to Dream though, they were able to weed out most of the trialists based on their age. They wanted kids around the ages of ten and eleven to join the academy. Africa has such a large population of highly motivated soccer players who spent hours and hours of time playing street soccer. The opportunity to help these talents are very slim, however, causing a lot of players coming from disparate backgrounds to do anything possible to succeed even if it meant lying about their age. Due to poverty and the lack of opportunities, many of these African soccer players lie about their age in a desperate search for a better life out of poverty.

This age cheating problem has continued to plague soccer in Africa because of the desperation of these players. For Right to Dream though, they were able to eliminate the most 'adults', who already had a full-grown beard and with the deepest voices yet claiming to be ten years old. After these obvious eliminations, they now turned to the best talent among the last people standing. Week by week they would let some people go until only twenty of us were left. We were the cream of the crop, but they only needed ten players. The stakes were high for both the players and Right to Dream. For the players, failure to be part of the academy would mean that they had to go back to living in poverty and having no future ahead. For Right to Dream, well, they must get it right. If they want the cream of the crop, then they must consider all the factors and pick the best to represent the academy.

CHAPTER 7

The Tryout

We must accept finite disappointment, but never lose infinite hope—
Martin Luther King, Jr.

We only had money for two tickets to make it out to Dawu for the final tryout. Since my Uncle Evans was coming with me, I sat on his lap on the way there, so he could use the other ticket on the way back. The whole journey from Kaneshie to Dawu took us about four hours as the passengers kept getting on and off the crowded bus. A few minutes after we got there, Kay and his dad also showed up. I was very happy to see Kay and vice versa. We realized that we had to stick together and help each other through this daunting task of getting a scholarship among over two hundred competitors. This number might seem slightly exaggerated but could be possible as players were coming in and out of the tryouts each week. My Uncle Evans said a few hellos to some of the Right to Dream staff members and left with Kay's dad. Although I was feeling a little sad and worried after my uncle left, the sight of Andy Farrant heading towards our direction changed my mood.

A familiar face is always good at a tryout stage. He shook our hands and said congratulations to us for making it this far. He told us to work hard during this crucial month of our lives. At this point, the players that were scouted all over Ghana had now trickled down into Dawu. We all got into conversing with each other and created a huge uproar of noise in the compound. The players that were scouted from Accra mostly spoke Ga, the second official language of the capital with English being the first. The players from the Ashanti region spoke Akan/Twi, then there were players from the northern part of Ghana who spoke Dagbani and players from the central region of Ghana who spoke Fante. The players from Accra had a little bit of the upper hand in language because of the different languages spoken in Accra since most people from all walks of Ghana migrate to Accra for a better job.

As a result, Accra became a melting pot for different dialects/ languages. Coming from Accra, I spoke Ga, Akan/Twi, Fante, and some Hausa, so I was able to converse with some of the tryout players that spoke those languages. Our loud conversation was cut short by the sight of four white men and two black men, all neatly dressed, who introduced themselves as the staff of the Right to Dream Academy.

Tom Vernon, the director of the academy, cleared his throat and welcomed all of us. He then congratulated us for making it this far and talked a little bit about what they were looking for and the structure of the tryouts. He finished by introducing the rest of the staff members, the three white staff members were: Gareth Henderby, Andy Farrant, Joe Mulberry, and the two black staff members were: Samuel Mawuena and Ben Adjei. They all shared a few words and encouraged us to get to bed early for an early start of the tournament the next morning.

'Get some rest tonight and see you all bright and early for the start of the justify tomorrow.' Tom closed the ceremony and we were escorted to our various rooms.

When I think of 'justify,' I quickly remember the trials that God's servants had to go through before they became successful. It is a term that suggests the idea of proving oneself faithful to God in the face of many tests. This biblical reference is a testament to Ghana's belief in God and the rampant growth of religious activities in Ghana. Pretty much every business building in Ghana has a reference to God in its name: God Is Good Salon, God Bless Auto Shop, God Will Provide Taxi Service, God Is the Answer Food Stand. Regarding 'justify' in sports, Ghanaians coined the term to shows the idea of proving you're better than your peers. All the children who came to the tryouts were undoubtedly good, but Right to Dream needed to find the best out of all of us.

There were ten scholarship spots available for over two hundred children, all of us bristling with talent and determined to grab an opportunity to transform our lives. Despite the pressure, I tried to shut out the distraction and focus on why I was at the tryouts. I often sat on my bed reading scriptures from the Bible and praying as often as possible to ask for God's help. I saw all the other kids at the tryouts praying to God or Allah as well. I often wondered whether God would listen to all of us and grant us our request or whether He would let the best talent win without any intervention. In either case, I was certain that Right to Dream Academy couldn't give scholarships to each trialist and that God's intervention only meant that He loves some people more than others.

The first day of the tryout was intense. This was not the first tryout I'd had in Ghana. When I was eight, I got the opportunity to attend tryouts with Feyenoord Academy and Ajax Academy. At each tryout, I had made it to the final day, but I failed to make the final cut. I would get close and then they would crush my spirit with their rejection speech. When Ajax Academy and Feyenoord Academy came into the scene, everyone in Ghana wanted to play for them. I was among the many young Ghanaian children who wanted to make it in life through soccer.

Feyenord Academy[ii] passed on me because they felt I was too small and didn't see any growth potential physically and mentally in myself. It was a decision that would come back to haunt them in a few years. Ajax on the other hand just didn't pick me at the final tryout. They basically said I was not good enough to earn a scholarship with them. Each time I got rejected, I never gave up on hope. I would pick myself up and work even harder to get ready for the next opportunity.

This time, with Right to Dream Academy, I was determined to make it all the way in the tryout. We were put into different groups, and we had about twelve players in each group. We started off with a fifteen-minute warm up, then we did a few passing drills and went straight into six vs six small-sided games. Everything was going well with the passing drills until we went to the small-sided games. Over the years, I had developed my game to be more of a passer than a dribbler. I had great technique in passing, from short to long range passing. However, at the tryout, anytime I passed to a teammate, they start to dribble. I would work very hard to win the ball back and when I passed the ball to another teammate, they start to also dribble. It was hard to communicate with them especially the players from the north who spoke Dagbani.

I felt a little disconnected because I was doing all the hard work but not on the same page with the players on my team. I got mad at my teammates and started to demand the ball at the top of my voice. It still didn't help. Kay was not on my team, but I could tell from glancing at the field next to us that he was having a better experience than me because he was a forward. After the six vs six small-sided games, I had a brief conversation with Kay, and he told me he'd scored a couple of goals.

I expressed my unhappiness with my team, and he told me to not worry but to keep working hard. I took his words to heart and our next game was a different experience. We were playing Kay's team. I changed my defensive central mid to a more attacking role, using my vision and passing technique to rip through their defense. I scored three goals in that small-sided game and felt a little more confident in my game. Things started to go well for me from then on. I was reading and intercepting a lot of passes from Kay's team.

After the small-sided games, we got a lunch break and a few hours of rest before we left for the next round of the tryouts later that day. As we got back to our rooms, we took a shower and we ended up in different groups. You could see the northern region players in their little circle, talking in Dagbani, a language I had no idea existed.

Our Ashanti region people also gravitated to each other and expressed concerns about the tryouts. The Accra players, including myself and Kay, were worried too, as we engaged in our conversation speaking Ga. We talked about how the tryouts were going so far, and the things we needed to improve to impress the coaches. There were about forty of us in each group, and like magnets, we all became attracted to the group that shared the most or same connection of language as we spoke.

The next round was all about playing full-field scrimmages. This was not new to us as we all grew up playing full-field in our local colt teams. The field was a frightening sight. There were white plastic chairs lined up around the field with each coach holding a clipboard and a pen. We were put into our teams, and in different positions. I took the central mid-field position as expected. I was smaller than most kids on my team due to poverty and malnutrition which stunted my growth. Millions of children in developing countries are stunted in growth through malnutrition by the time they reach the age of seven. Although stunting can affect a child's cognitive abilities as well as their focus and concentration, I felt that I was the brains of my tryout team.

Most of these players just wanted to dribble at every part of the field. Defenders would start dribbling at the back and they would lose possession and get scored on. A few moments later, they would do the same—déjà vu. For most of the players, dribbling was their way to impress the coaches. They felt that if they were able to dribble the entire team and score, they would be noticed and be selected. I, on the other hand, was more of a passer than a dribbler. I always looked to pass and became more of an assistant to goal scoring opportunities than scoring. I had my fair share of goals though. My favorite types of goals were the ones where I would link up with the forward and slide the ball past the goalkeepers as they slid on the ground to block my shot. As the tryouts progressed, Tom moved players around and I ended up on the same team as Kay. I was very happy because I knew the type of runs Kay made and we were also used to our one-two combinations instead of hogging the ball like most of the players on our initial respective teams.

We played as if we were on the same wavelength, playing to the same tune of music and dancing to the same beat. It was the best we both played all day. We were dominant in the game. I scored one goal and had an assist for Kay, who scored two goals that game. We were flying with confidence at this point as we saw the pen moving on the clipboard anytime we would conjure up a bit of magic on the field.

At the end of the first week of tryouts, ten players were sent home. We all knew we needed to work hard and step up our game to maintain our spot in the tryouts. We all became very worried, and we got the message—people will go home every weekend. The following weekend saw more than ten people home, and once again, Kay and I stayed put. By the time we got to the final week of the tryouts, we were down to twenty players.

At this point, all twenty of us had formed a closely-knit group, breaking all the barriers that our different dialects rigidly instituted. We were able to learn a thing or two from each other to hold conversations and we would fall back on the little broken English we knew as back up to keep the conversation going. We became like a family, and even though Kay was my closest friend throughout the tryouts, I formed strong bonds with other people from Tamale and Kumasi as well. This gradual bond helped us to work well together on and off the field.

The twenty players that were left at this point included: me; Kay Boateng my teammate from Rot-Weiss; Razak Nuhu, a very technical and smart left back from Tamale; Thomas Boakye, a very strong central midfielder from Kumasi; Aminu Peci, a five foot pacey forward from Tamale (a pacey is someone who moves very quickly or fast paced); Rashid Muhammed, a very smart and technical attacking midfielder from Tamale; James Nortie, a goalkeeper from Accra with a very big span; Abdul Baba, a very skillful winger from Kumasi; Amos Obour, a strong and athletic defender from Tamale; Richie Tetteh, a quick center back from Accra; Abdul Waris, a very strong and intelligent forward from Tamale; Ember Power, a pacey winger from Kumasi; Frimpong Oreba, a goalkeeper from Cape Coast; Atobra Ampadu, an intelligent center back from Accra; Emmanuel Nana Akyen, a short, skillful and versatile midfielder from Accra; Oscar Umar, a tall lanky defender from Tamale; Mystro Pele, a physically strong midfielder from Accra; Issahaku Lukman, a tall defender from Tamale; Kingsley Aboakye, a midfielder from Accra; Francis 'Boti' Kobla, a fast, stocky forward from Accra.

Who was next to go home? This question became the topic of our conversations during our breaks and the thought of it would keep most of us up at night. The final week of tryouts was very intense. Every player was determined to do whatever it took to grab one of the scholarships. Players flew into tackles to win possession and forwards received a whack from the back as they tried to turn to shoot on goal. It was an intense week filled with great performances all over the field.

On the last day of the tryouts, we were told we would play Nungua FC, an U14 colt team from Accra. Even though they were older than us, we were all excited by the opportunity to play. We were put into two teams and we were told that each team would play half of the full game. However, some players would be rotated around to play both halves. This was the final test of our fate. We were all excited, yet worried as it would mean that some players from the twenty players left would not make the cut to get the limited full scholarships.

As the day finally arrived, Tom talked to us once again and told us he was very proud of us for getting this far. He mentioned that we should relax and enjoy the final game and give him our best soccer game as possible. When Nungua FC arrived at Dawu, all twenty of us warmed up together to get ready to play. Tom started reading off the list of players for the first half. Kay was among the eleven names that were mentioned. Each name came with a bit of shock and surprise—my name was not on the list. I began to get very worried and concluded that my run for the scholarship was over. Kay made it through at least, I thought to myself as I made my way to sit on the wooden bench next to the field.

The first half was back and forth and looked to be heading off to a stalemate as Nungua FC's physicality seemed to match the technicality of our first team.

'Fifi, warm up,' Tom instructed from his chair next to our bench.

I jogged up and down the sideline and did a few stretches. Tom told me to go in for Boakye, the midfielder from Kumasi. It was about ten minutes left of the first half of the game. As soon as I got into the game, I received a ball from our right back, Amos, and laid it off first time to our right winger Ember Power. Always play simple and take care of the ball: these were among some of the words that went through my head when I went to the game. Ember held the ball with his defender at his back. I created some space for myself by making a quick run behind my defender. Ember saw my run and passed the ball to me in the space. I quickly switched a diagonal ball to Baba, our left winger, who was able to beat his defender with his fast step-overs and sent a high cross in the box. Kay went up for the header, but the goalkeeper came out of the goal and punched the ball. As I was running towards the opponents' goal, I saw the ball coming in my direction. As the ball made its way towards me, my initial thought was to receive it with my chest and look to pass.

However, seeing the goalkeeper out of his goal, I decided to go for it. What was the worst that could happen? At least I tried something audacious. I went for it first time with a volley and I saw the ball in the back of the net. The whole field went into a big uproar of clapping from both benches except for the coaches, who were too busy writing on their clipboard. I was very happy at that moment. We went to the first half with a one-nil lead, thanks to my wonderful volley from a distance. I would go on to play the rest of the second half as well.

The second half started off with the same intensity as the first half but saw the opponents wearing out as we poured on them with our new fresh team including myself. Our performance in the second half was nothing short of outstanding. We absolutely dominated the game, restricted the opposition from their rhythm and proved how talented we were. I ended with two assists in that game and Kay, Aminu, Waris and Baba would go on to score the rest of our goals in our five-one thumping of Nungua FC.

Nungua FC had a young forward by the name David Accam, who scored their only goal. David Accam missed the opportunity to come to the final tryouts because he was sick and failed to play in the Right to Dream tournament that brought us to Dawu. David, who caught the attention of all the staff would end up at the academy a week after the final tryout. I played well in that game, distributing passes, combining plays, and breaking down the opposition with my 'hiding passes' or 'no look passes.'

'Hiding passing' or 'no look passing' is a creative form of passing where you look one way to deceive the opponent and then you pass the ball the other way. I was bristling with pure confidence after that game and was sure, by the end of the tryout, that my performance had been good enough to make the final cut. After the game, we had lunch and we were all told to shower and pack our bags. The moment we'd all been waiting for had finally arrived as we waited for the final decisions from the staff.

We all went to our rooms and found a quiet place to pray to God for help. We then grouped together in one room and tried our best to cast determined looks of confidence that we would be among the chosen few to earn a scholarship. With no family member in sight and no cell phones to call our various homes for moral support, we stood in the room full of confidence, excitement, and nervousness. The Right to Dream staff were in one room with the door closed, discussing our final fate. They were in the room for a long time. At least it seemed like a very long time to us. We could tell it was a tough decision for them. It was very much nerve-racking for us.

It seemed like the plans had changed behind the scenes as they looked to take more players than they initially planned. Tom came out of the room and summoned us. He explained that they only had nine spots for the scholarship available to offer that day and some of the players needed further review and would come back for a week to try out for the final spot. He said that they would have individual meetings with us and let us know where we stood in their decision. He went back to their room and they closed the door again.

At that time, we were pooping our pants. Where does each of us stand now? We started to discuss among ourselves and began to worry some more. Joe Mulberry came and asked Razak to accompany him to the room.

They were in there for a long time until Razak came out with a team tracksuit. With a big smile on his face, he told us he had been offered a scholarship. We congratulated him and expressed how happy we were for him, but we knew there were only eight spots available now for nineteen players. A few minutes later, Baba and then Aminu followed and they both came back with outfits, indicating they both got full scholarships. Then it was my turn. What would my fate be?

Am I going to be told that I had to come back for a further tryout, or I didn't make the cut at all? As confident as I was before, I was honestly very frightened to hear my fate. I was nervous and shaking from head to toe. As soon as I walked into the room, they could all sense that I was very nervous. Andy was sitting there with a big smile on his face as if to tell me to relax. Tom cleared his throat,

'Congratulations Fifi, you made the final cut. You are one of the nine players to be offered a full scholarship.' Those words quickly brought me to tears of joy. Mama, I made it!

They told me how proud they were of me and how intelligent I was on and off the field. They said they saw me going places, but I needed to put in more work because of my size. When I came out of the room, I was half in tears and half smiling. A lot of the other players thought I didn't make the cut but were surprised when they saw the outfit hidden behind my back. They congratulated me as well and at this point, I started to hope for the best for Kay. He'd been exceptional throughout the whole tryout, but the spots were quickly filling up. Then it was James, Nana, Rashid, Kay, and Waris in that order. When Kay came back with his outfit, we were ecstatic and overwhelmed with joy.

It was one of the most beautiful moments of my life, knowing that my good friend and teammate had also made the cut. We were extremely happy to the point where we almost forgot our other friends whose fates were not so great. The following players were asked to come back for further review: Atobra, Boakye, Amos, and Oscar. These players would end up getting full scholarships after their first week of tryouts. We would become the second-generation group of the academy.

Like the first generation, almost all of us would find fame and fortune playing professional soccer and acquiring college degrees in one of the best schools in the US. We would arguably become the most successful generation of the academy. Unfortunately, the rest of the players did not make the cut at all. Finally, Tom and the rest of the staff came out for their final closing comments. They congratulated all of us once again and encouraged the boys who didn't make the cut to continue to work hard and to not lose hope.

At this point, they were all dejected and their hope had turned to despair. It was a crushing blow to them, as they sat with their heads down. Those of us that got full scholarships, as well as the ones that were required for further review, were instructed to report to the academy in two weeks. I left the tryouts with so much happiness, so much to tell my family and so much to improve on if I wanted to be a consistent player at the academy. My family was very happy to hear that I made the cut. I gave the rest of the money that they gave us for transport and as pocket money to my grandmother.

That night they prepared my favorite Ghanaian dish: Jolof rice with chicken. My grandma's jollof is the best. The recipe includes onions, vegetable oil, tomatoes, pepper, curry powder, garlic powder, ground ginger, rice, vegetables and water. I helped by fetching in large plastic containers of water since we didn't have a tap. It was the first time in many months that we ate chicken. We only ate chicken on special occasions and that night was certainly a celebration for us. As news spread through our neighborhood, I became a local celebrity and people would wave and stop me to congratulate me over and over. Most people told me not to forget about them when I made it big. Others took a wiser approach by telling me to always remember where I came from and keep working hard.

Me with my uncles Eric, Evans, and Emma
(From left to right)

Me with my grandma, Elizabeth
during his last visit to Ghana

Me and my Mum, Anna in Ghana

Me with my grandma, Elizabeth, my mom, Anna,
and my three siblings, Betty, Rejoice and Samuel

The Kaneshie Market, where I sold kerosene

The team and I at Rotweiss, when Andy Farrant
became our coach for the tournament

Tom addressing my team at the academy after a game.

Andy and me in Ghana

(From left to right) Atobra, me, and C. Nortcy
leaving to the U.S. in 2007

(Pictured with my shirt off) I am enjoying some
time with the boys at Right to Dream Academy

I am with Abu and Razak in England, during our
time at Fulham Academy

When I was playing
soccer at Dunn School

Showing my award for academic excellence with
Michael Tetteh at Dunn School

Graduating from Dunn School in 2010

Me with my host family, Darol, Janet, Katie and
Brian Joseff

With my team at Santa Barbara Soccer Club after
winning a trophy

Running out at UCSB before our game

Here's me doing the robot dance after I scored

Graduating from UCSB

After signing for Columbus Crew

Me in action for Columbus Crew

When I volunteered at OrphanAid Africa

In the Ghanaian Newspaper when I
started Fifi Soccer Foundation

With the children at Fifi Soccer Foundation

Spending some time at the beach in Ghana with the children
at Fifi Soccer Foundation

Me with the children at the Foundation when they
visited the Kwame Nkrumah Museum in Accra, Ghana

Enjoying the sunset as I embrace the dream I have to
inspire hope to children

Many thanks to the Santa Barbara Community for their
continuous support towards the Fifi Soccer Foundation

CHAPTER 8

Second generation

Struggle is a never-ending process. Freedom is never really won; you earn it and win it in every generation—Coretta Scott King

When we returned to the academy, we were placed in our rooms. The room was twice as big than the one I was used to at my grandparent's apartment. It had two big windows and four bunkbeds. Although there were eight people that shared the same room, we had our own beds and mattresses. I was very happy to be able to sleep in comfort without being worried about flies and the sounds of rats running on the roof. In fact, I had never seen a bunkbed before, so I kept my eyes busily looking around the room.

I was not the only one. Everyone sat on their beds with a look of disbelief and excitement. We met the first-generation group. Tom quickly paired us with the first-generation players, so they could be mentors to us. I was initially paired with Michael Sai, a tall, bulky goalkeeper from Accra and then moved under Steven Osei, a midfielder with the first touch of gold after Michael left the academy with reasons unknown. The 'mentorship' was more about us washing their clothes and running errands for them. When the tap was not working, we would walk about twenty yards from the academy to a nearby well to fetch water for ourselves and for our first-generation mentors.

We drew water from the well with the practiced ease that came from doing the same thing three times a day, every day. We eased the rope through our hands until the plastic tub emerged from the lip of the well, then decanted the clear liquid into a large bucket. Not a drop was spilled. By our feet, chickens pecked at the ground, oblivious to a puppy that wanted to join in the game.

I learned a lot from my mentors as well. Michael always offered to help me work on my shooting goals technique. Since he was a goalkeeper, I would get a bag of soccer balls and just continue to shoot at him while he offered critiques about my shooting. Steven, on the other hand, had the best ability to pass and receive a ball. He always played with so much grace and flair that he made soccer seem effortless. I asked him many questions about my passing, and he worked with me on my long passing range.

The schedule at the academy was tough. A typical day at the academy began with an hour of doing our chores at 6 am such as sweeping, cleaning our room, compound, bathroom and washing the dishes from the night before. Then we would do our morning worship, praying to God and singing praises and dancing to the sound of singing and drumming. At 7.30 am, we had an hour and a half of morning training, followed by breakfast, returning to the academy to take a shower before having three and a half hours of school. We would then break for lunch, have a rest, and do a second training around 5 pm. We ended the day with a few more hours of homework, dinner, and then lights out by 10 pm.

We set aside time very early in the morning to do our own personal training before chores to work on the areas of our game that needed to be improved. We followed this routine for five days a week and then played games on Saturday, resting on Sunday. Lastly, we would do game analysis with Tom about our performance from the previous game.

I loved these video analyses because it was a great way to see and learn from our mistakes. The first-generation players set the tone for the second-generation in terms of opportunities in Europe and the United States. Three weeks after we got to Dawu, two of the first-generation players, King Osei Gyan and Waid Ibrahim, were awarded full scholarships to the United States to study at Dunn School in Los Olivos. A year after they left, Michael Tetteh and Bello Alhassan followed suit, going to Dunn School. This was not just a testament to the success of Right to Dream, but also gave us hope about the possibility of our future in the US if we continued to work hard.

Other than the United States route, we also gained some confidence to play in Europe when three of the first-generation players—Samuel Mensah, Godfred Saka and Telly Shaze—were invited for a tryout with the U16 Academy sides of Everton FC and Newcastle United in England. These opportunities really boosted our confidence about our career paths through the academy—whether playing in England or going to school in the United States. I had a lot of really good days at the academy.

Ever since I joined the academy, I was eager to learn and to grow. I looked for creative ways to improve my game including running up the hills with some of my teammates early in the morning or working on passing with Steven or my shooting with Michael. I asked a lot of questions. My relationship with Andy became very strong. He always offered a word of encouragement and advice to improve my game.

Andy's parents became my sponsors at the academy. They sent me jerseys and some pocket money to help support my family, and I will forever be grateful for everything they did for me and continue to do for me in my life. I had the best days during my five-year tenure at the academy. I was a regular starter and only started off the bench on two occasions that I could remember. I scored a lot of goals and assisted a lot of goals as well. I had so many great performances, including the time when I received a pass and without looking, I gave a backheel through pass to Boakye who hit the post. One of my best memories was when we played Feyenoord Academy at their home grounds in Gomoa Fete, a six-hour journey from Dawu. Feyenoord Academy, our only rival academy at the time, had a lot of really good players from all over the country and their selection was as rigorous as that of Right to Dream.

I also had a bit of a personal pain against Feyenoord academy since they didn't select me at their tryout. They say, 'revenge is the dessert best served cold' and I wanted revenge on them for passing me up at the final tryout decision. The week leading up to playing Feyenoord Academy was full of focus and hard work on my part. I did four times of personal training, instead of my usual three times a week on top of our regular training routine at the academy.

I felt very fit and ready to play in that game. The moment I've been waiting for finally arrived. Tom gave us a whole speech that week about the importance of making sure we do our best in that game. The game was more of a bragging right for us, but for Tom, it was a great opportunity to use our performance to attract investors for the academy. He would be able to say, look at the facts, we beat Feyenoord Academy and we beat all the local teams, we have the best talent in Ghana.

Indeed, the game was nothing short of the best display of talent in Ghana at the time. Tom and some of our staff took their seat next to the main director of Feyenoord Academy to enjoy the game. Both directors sat with big smiles on their face, confident of the team they had assembled. Like Feyenoord Academy, the players that Tom had assembled had spent thousands of hours playing in the streets with our colt teams before we made it to the academy, and the experience showed from both teams when we took the field. The pressure was on. We took our positions on the beautiful, big, artificially-turfed field, waiting for the whistle to blow.

I started in midfield with Abu Muhammed, a left-footed midfielder who would become one of the best players at the academy. Abu and I had different playing styles, but we spoke the same language, and understood each other's playing style. Our consistent partnership in the middle of the field made it very easy for us and could even see what the other was thinking when they had possession of the ball.

The game started in an intense fashion, with each team being masters of possession. One team had the ball for some time and once they lost possession, they chased the opposing team like a headless chicken to get it back. Feyenoord needed to score to impress their director since they were playing at home. They pushed forward aggressively with each possession they gained after their director started to make gestures for his need of a goal.

Time and again, we swatted them back and looked dangerous on the counter attack with Nana and David missing goal scoring opportunities. The Feyenoord midfielders had just a little luck getting the ball past Abu and me in midfield. We closed them down quickly and kept the ball when we gained possession. I got one ball from Razak on the left, and I hit and sixty-yard switch ball to Amos who was wide open on the other side because Feyenoord had shifted their lines to the left side to put pressure on us.

There were cheers and claps from our coaching staff and a thumbs up from Tom after I gave that switch ball. Tom would go on to highly praise me during our game analysis on that pass and my ability to pick those passes at crucial moments of the game. After that, the game became a back and forth interchange of possessions and shots. As the first half ended, we poured on the pressure against Feyenoord Academy and conjured a moment of magic in the first half. I got the ball, and looking at the goal from thirty yards, I decided to have a shot at goal. As the ball pierced through their center backs on the way towards goal, our forward, Aminu, a five-foot, two-inch super-fast striker from

Tamale, latched onto the ball and managed to slot it past Feyenoord's goalkeeper, prompting wild celebrations from us. Despite many attempts from Feyenoord, we held on to win the game one-nil, a huge victory.

We now enjoyed the reputation as the first team to beat Feyenoord on their home soil, making Right to Dream Academy the academy to beat in Ghana. We all stayed in Dawu until the end of May and then we packed our bags to head home for the summer. In the months since joining the academy, we had fast become a tight-knit group. Despite coming from different parts of Ghana and speaking different languages, we grew to understand each other and learned to appreciate our differences. Other than being divided culturally and religiously, almost all of us came from similar backgrounds.

Like most things in life, my failures overshadowed my many successes at Right to Dream Academy. When I look back, I realize that my failures were the ones that opened the doors for me to enjoy the most important success in my life. One of my biggest failures at Right to Dream Academy was the time when I got injured in the spring of 2005. It was my first injury at the academy, one that would sideline me for a few months. We were playing a team in Accra, and we were dominating that game. There was a fifty-fifty ball between me and one of their midfielders. We both slid for the ball and his studs got the inside of my right foot. I was down for a few minutes and thought it was just a bruise. I signaled to the referee to give me a second to get up. After a few minutes, I was up on my feet and the referee instructed the game to continue. As I was limping back to receive a ball, I could feel something wasn't right with my foot. I felt a sharp shooting pain down my foot. It was so painful to even stand. As I went down again, I signaled our coach, Ben Adjei, to take me off.

After I was escorted off the field, they took me to the nearest hospital for an x-ray and they found out I had fractured my ankle. It was one of the painful comebacks from injury of my life. No stranger to injuries, I thought I would be back within a few weeks. The first two weeks went by and I was still in a cast. A few weeks after that, I was cleared to play. I started jogging and everything seemed to head in the right direction for a full recovery. However, after I progressed from jogging and slowly eased my way into practice, I hurt my ankle again. I worked with our physiotherapist again and again but didn't see any improvement. I went for another MRI and it showed that everything was fine.

Whenever I returned to play, I still felt the pain in my ankle. Did I rush to play too soon? Am I really that injured or was it all in my head? I would go to practice one day and miss the following days after that. This time, they thought I was faking it. I missed a lot of practices and games throughout that period. My touches were very rusty, and I lost all confidence in the sport.

When I went out and try to play, again, I would be lost in the game as I kept limping throughout the practice session, prompting my teammates to encourage me to sit out. Everything felt very strange at the academy. Whenever I didn't finish my chores on time, I would get punished for that. I became the talk of the academy, and I felt that everyone and everything was against me. During that same time, my uncle visited the academy out of the blue and I thought the staff at the academy had complained to my family back home.

Far from it, he came to inform me about the sudden death of my grandfather. I lost it after hearing that news. I was already living a difficult life at the academy and the news just made everything worse. I told the coaching staff the tragic news about my family and they gave me a leave of absence. I went home to attend his funeral; it was one of the most difficult times of my life. Seeing my grandmother and all the family members in tears really made my heart ache. At that time, Tom was out of the country, raising money and looking for professional tryout opportunities for us in Europe. When he returned and heard about my consecutive missing of practice, he was very disappointed in me. He got reports that I was faking my injury to avoid practice and that I had developed a negative attitude towards work.

In the past, whenever I saw Tom, he would smile at me and ask how things were going. He usually had words of encouragement for me to keep working hard and reminded me that I was getting close to a great opportunity. This time, when I saw him, he didn't even want to make eye contact with me. He had a look of discontent on his face and he barely spoke to me during his two weeks that he was around.

I had a lot of conversations with Kay, Razak, and David. These were the three players who were playing with so much confidence at the time. Not too long after he left, Kay, Razak, and David got passports and left for a tryout at Newcastle United. I was happy for them, especially Kay because he was my closest friend at the academy. However, I was very disappointed in myself for not being in the conversation of the top players at the academy at the time. Before this whole situation, I was always included in the top three players. A few weeks later, Nana was offered the opportunity to travel to the US to join King, Waid, Bello, and Michael at Dunn School. I went from being at the top of the conversation to not being in the conversation at all. It was a very emotional and heartbreaking time for me at that time.

Andy was gone for a few months to the UK to complete his coaching license. When he returned, he heard about reports of my 'bad' behavior. He expressed his heartfelt disappointment about my change of attitude and my plummeting performance.

'What happened to you, Fifi? You are losing out on all these opportunities. Tom and the staff are fed up with your behavior and you might be seeing your way out of the academy,' he said in a tone of disappointment and shame.

Those words really shook me to my core. I'm going to be kicked out of the academy? My mind was racing at this point. Was I faking my injury? I had always been one of the most consistent players at the academy. Now, I had a choice to give up hope and go back to my family or I could work through this injury and come out stronger. I chose to go with the latter.

I had come so far and was not ready to turn back. I started to plan in my head about what I needed to do. I was optimistic that I had what it took to come out on top of the situation. My whole life had been shaped with bitter life experiences of poverty, pain, and rejection. I realized that my strength came from my hard work, my strong mindset to cope with bad situations, and my perseverance to achieve my goals. I was down but I was never broken. I could make a turnaround. I needed to make a change.

It was not an easy turnaround, but I was determined to make a positive change to all the negative perceptions that tarnished my image in the academy. I started working with the physiotherapist again and I slowly progressed from jogging to running and then to sprinting. Every time I felt the pain in my ankle, I just pressed on. I was determined to overcome that pain and to get back to playing consistently again.

One week later, I was back in full swing. I came back to my usual routine of personal training on top of our regular schedule at the academy and I began to get stronger physically and mentally.

That weekend, I started off the bench in our game. It was the first time I had started off the bench when I was healthy to play. I had lost my spot to a trialist by the name Felix, a tall and strong midfielder from Accra. The first half was an even game of both teams pressing to get an early goal. We had the most possessions but were finding it difficult to break down the opponent's defense. As the game progressed to the twenty minutes into the first half, Felix got the first goal from a cross.

He was riding high in confidence and perhaps thought he had taken my spot after the game. The game ended one-nil at half time. The second half started with almost the same line-up, and I was still on the bench. I kept looking at our coach for the opportunity to play but no signal came. As I sat there patiently with the clock ticking, I wondered whether I was ever going in. I knew that this game was my opportunity to announce to everyone that I was back in full swing.

Finally, I got the nod to take out Felix and join Abu in mid-field. I had not played with Abu for over two months now and it didn't take us long to get back in sync with each other. Five minutes after I got into the game, I scored our second goal through a succession of passes in mid-field and a link up play with Waris. When I slotted the ball past the oncoming goalkeeper, it was a major confidence boost for me. I had scored many goals in the academy, but this time was different.

I celebrated the goal like I scored the greatest goal in a champions league game. My teammates saw what that goal meant to me and they all came with big hugs as if to say welcome come back, Fifi. We went on to win the game five-nil, thanks to my goal and three assists. It was a great day for me. Unfortunately, Tom and Andy were not there at that time. I wished they had been there, and I hoped they heard about the new me. The following week of practice was a confidence boost as well. I trained extra hard to catch up to game speed with my teammates. I felt like my old self again. I started our next game and the ones that would follow. I was back to myself, combining, creating and winning tackles in mid-field.

I played the full game and the games that would follow suit. My confidence was back and through consistent playing, I was back to playing at my best. That summer, Tom brought a couple of scouts from Fulham Academy[iii]to watch us train for a week. They were impressed with my playing from the first day. Tom was very impressed too and happy that I was back in action again. He was smiling at me again and encouraged me to keep up with my good work. On their last day, we played a game for the scouts. We played the U20 team of Liberty Professionals, a professional team in the Ghana Premier League. We were around fourteen years old at the time and still competed against them.

Their physicality was no match to our quick possession play and combination through mid-field. This time, we played a diamond in mid-field and it was me, Abu and Razak, who used to play left back. Tom wanted to see how well we played together in mid-field and we were excellent. The game ended on a two-all draw, but it was a game that we dominated possession and deserved the victory. After that game, Tom called me, Abu and Razak and told us that the scouts from Fulham were very impressed with the way we played. Since we were not eighteen years yet, they invited us to a tryout with their academy team.

We were very excited about this opportunity and when the news spread through the academy about our opportunity, they rejoiced with us and knew it was well deserved. We were in fact, the best players at the academy at the time. That same year when we had our end of year awards party, I won the overall best player at the academy. It was a crowning achievement for me, and I was very proud to receive such an amazing award amid all the great players at the academy. A few months back, I was the same person that was shunned by everyone at the academy. I was injured; I had lost my grandfather; I had lost my confidence. I lost everything. One thing I knew I didn't lose was my hope. So true that sometimes it's better to take one step back and then two steps forward. I believed in myself and held on to my hope of success at the academy.

CHAPTER 9

Fulham Academy

Walk on with hope in your heart, and you'll never walk alone—Shah Rukh Khan

In the summer of 2006, I was walking on cloud nine as we departed for England for a tryout at the Fulham Academy. When I got the opportunity to go and play in England, I was ecstatic. All my hard work and prayers had come true. There were millions of young African players like me, who grew up fantasizing about playing in Europe and now, I had the opportunity to live that dream. It was the first time I owned a passport. It was the first time I travelled outside of Ghana. When we arrived in England, I was shocked to see how clean the streets were, how people observed traffic rules, how people didn't travel for a mile or two to get water, and there was no rationing of electricity.

These weren't the only things that I marveled at. The house we stayed at was very nice, very different from the cramped and spartan conditions that I grew up in Abossey Okai. I had my own bedroom, and my own flat screen TV to operate. This was a new luxury I was very thankful to enjoy. I was also very impressed with the high-end training facility at Fulham Academy. The soccer field was beautiful. The grass was very green and neatly cut to the perfect layer for soccer. The all-you-could-eat buffet at lunchtime was a revelation for me as well. Even though I was never hungry at Right to Dream Academy, I certainly had never experienced that kind of abundance in my life. It brought tears to my eyes as I saw how other people lived on the other side of the Atlantic Ocean, compared to the chaotic life back in Ghana.

Other than all the things I marveled at, I also had some adjusting to do like operating elevators and having hot-water showers. I didn't know how to turn the water on to the perfect temperature, and either turned it too hot or too cold. Another adjustment was using a fork and knife at the dinner table. Before Right to Dream Academy, I mostly ate with my hand. At Right to Dream Academy, I had used my hand, spoon, or fork. At Fulham Academy, I had to learn how to use a fork and knife to eat without using my hand. Forks and knives fell out of my hand onto the floor as I tried to cut a piece of steak. However, this new luxury didn't take me long to adjust to.

Our first training with Fulham Academy U16 was a success. We did a few passing drills, crossing, and finishing. Then we went on to play small-sided games. I was in the same team as Abu and Razak, so it felt like back at the Right to Dream Academy. I was spraying balls from left to right and combining plays with Abu in mid-field. One of the key moments was the hard tackle I did on one of the players to win possession. It was a hard tackle and I thought I had broken his leg. After a few minutes of being on the ground, he was back on his feet and playing. I felt a sigh of relief as I didn't want my first training to end up with someone going to the hospital. After a couple of days, I became used to the players and got acclimatized to their style of play.

One of my fondest memories at Fulham was when we shared lunch breaks with the first team players at the time. We usually sat next to Clint Dempsey, who was playing at Fulham at the time. We were all surprised that he wasn't getting any playing time with the first team. He would often joke that 'another day, another dollar,' to express his mix feelings about not playing. After all, he would still make his money even if they didn't play him. Eventually, Dempsey gained a starting position and went on to scoring important goals to keep the team from relegation that year.

My success at Fulham ended when I fractured my left ankle in our game against Charlton FC. I was playing well in that game. In the opening five minutes, I almost scored off a corner. I made a fast run near the post when they drilled the ball across the goal, missing the inside of my foot narrowly as I tried to direct the ball to the back of the net. This early miss was followed by a succession of fifty-fifty tackles that I won for our team to put pressure on Charlton. We were dominating the first half until I got injured at the twenty-minute mark of the first half. We had a throw-in and I checked away with my defender and came toward the ball.

My first instinct was to pass it back to the thrower with the inside of my foot but at the last second, I changed my mind to turn with my left foot.

As I turned, the metal studs of my cleat caught in the soft grass and the next thing I heard was a snap. I immediately went down, and everyone could tell it was bad. I was in pain, the greatest physical pain I had felt in my whole life. They called an ambulance and I was escorted to the nearby hospital. When I woke up, I was in a cast at the hospital. I was down again, but this time was different. I got to the top of playing in Europe and I had to start all over again. I started to cry as soon as I saw some of my teammates and Andy at my hospital bedside. The team went on to beat Charlton three-one.

'Is it really bad?' I asked the doctor when he came to the room to check on me.

'You are going to be back playing in no time,' he replied with a smile on his face.

I felt as if some weight was lifted off my shoulders. If I could return to play, I thought to myself, I could deal with the recovery process. It was a long recovery process or at least it felt so. I was on crutches for a few months. While I was doing physical therapy at Fulham Academy, Razak and Abu were playing consistently. Being sidelined with an injury and watching your teammates play in games is one of the most painful things for every athlete.

Memories about my previous injury which turned everyone at Right to Dream against me crept through my mind, but this time I remained positive. I was determined to come out stronger and with a positive mindset. One of soccer's superstars, Zinedine Zidane, once said,

'I once cried because I had no shoes to play football with my friends, but one day I saw a man who had no feet, and I realized how rich I am.' When we are dealing with situations, we tend to think that the whole world is coming to get us. We become so absorbed in our circumstance that we fail to keep our hope for a better life. We should learn to overcome our misery by looking for ways to use our story to inspire others. I constantly reminded myself to remain positive and to look forward to working even harder when I got to play again.

That summer, we returned to Ghana as Fulham Academy went on vacation. I returned in a cast and worked extra hard after they took off my cast. A few weeks later I returned to full contact play, Tom returned to the academy and had a meeting with me, James, and Atobra. He had full scholarships from the US for us to further our education.

We were all very happy when we heard the news, but for me, it was one miracle after another. I was down at Fulham a couple of months ago and I was up ready for another exciting part of my life. God had been so good to me and I was thankful for every opportunity that came my way. I joined Waid, Michael, Bello, and Nana in California at Dunn School and James and Atobra headed off to the east coast. King had left California because he had turned eighteen a few months before and had signed a professional contract with Fulham FC. He was the first to sign a professional contract at the academy, a crowning achievement for him and the academy. The year was August 2007, and I was off to California to embark on my journey to acquire a better education—thanks to God, Right to Dream, and Dunn School.

CHAPTER 10

Coming to America

If we expect change, we must act on our hope every day until we have accomplished what we wanted—Christopher Goodman

Coming to America was an opportunity for me to fulfil my dream of acquiring a quality education, playing professional soccer, and being a mentor to young kids. I was drawn to America because of the ethos it carried—the land of the free and home to the brave. I learned about this American pride in all the American movies I got to watch in Ghana. Everybody wants freedom, and I guess I'd been brave enough to deal with all my past struggles, so I deserved to be in America.

I was also drawn to the American culture through the accent. I remember a few months before I came to America, a volunteer visited the Right to Dream Academy; his name was James Alba. I had the pleasure of meeting him and getting to know him. He was very kind to us and could tell he had a big heart. I was drawn by his accent, especially the way he pronounced water and better, a pronunciation so different from what we learned from our colonizers, the British. I asked him many questions about America and the standard of living, and I was sold by all the great responses he gave about America.

As a result, when Tom presented the opportunity to study at Dunn School, it was a no-brainer to grab it without thinking twice about it. I arrived in America in the summer of 2007 at LAX (Los Angeles) airport alone. Initially, I travelled with James and Atobra accompanied by one of the staff members at Right to Dream, Anna. When we arrived in New York, Anna went with James and Atobra to their respective high schools and I travelled alone to LAX. I would be met with Debbie, Waid, Bello, and Nana when I got to Los Angeles. For someone coming to a foreign land for at least a few years, I should be travelling with lots of luggage. However, I arrived at LAX with a small carry-on duffle bag that contained four shirts, three pairs of shorts, one pair of jeans and three athletics tracksuits. That was all I owned at the time, thanks to Right to Dream and my sponsors, John and Moira Farrant. It was great to see my fellow Ghanaians—Waid, Nana, and Bello at the airport. The sight of them made me feel at ease and felt like I was home.

'Okay Fifi, what color is your suitcase? We need to get that from baggage claim,' Debbie asked after I said hello and she gave me a big hug. 'I don't have any more bags. This is all I brought,' I replied sharply in my thick Ghanaian accent.

She had a look of surprise on her face, and quickly got the message: that's the way the other half of the world lives. Indeed, life is tough on the other side of the Atlantic Ocean. I was led to the parking lot into her car and off to the promised land—America. It didn't take me that long to experience my first teaching moment about the American culture. A few minutes after we drove off from the airport, Debbie told us that she needed to get gas. When she stopped at a gas station, I quickly got out of the car, wondering why my other fellow Ghanaians did not offer to help.

Debbie asked if I needed anything. 'No, I just want to help,' I humbly replied. Again, she was shocked and said, 'It's okay, I think I got it. I just need to fill the tank.' At this point, I was already at the back of the car, waiting for her to open the trunk so I could take out the cylinder to fill the gas.

In Ghana, we refer to the fuel we put in the car as 'petrol,' and we refer to 'gas' as what they put in the cylinder to cook. Most rich people in Ghana use gas stoves to cook their meals instead of the charcoal stove. So, when someone said they need gas, we assume the gas in the cylinder had run out and would take the empty cylinder to the nearest gas station to fill it up. I was dumbfounded when Debbie said she didn't need my help to get the gas, thinking she meant the gas was used to cook meals on the gas stove. You learn something new every day, right? I swallowed my shame and went back in the car. It was my first few minutes in America and I was already making mistakes and learning. This was going to be great—more learning to do; I loved it.

During my first few days, I was introduced to my host family, the Joseffs—Darol, Janet, and their two children Brian and Katie. The host family system was like when a family host a foreign exchange student for the period that they study abroad. In my case, they became my family for life.

I love this family to death. They have been so good to me ever since I came to America. I'm very thankful to have them in my life. The Joseffs are kind-hearted people, very loving and caring, and always there to help me through thick and thin. They bought me clothes, fed me, and helped me to get assimilated into the American culture. They were doctors, so obviously they took care of my health. Both doctors, Darol and Janet, presented a demeanor of hard work and humility.

Darol was very humble and caring and always there to listen to my troubles and offer solutions. I spent a lot of time with Darol. One of my favorite things I liked doing with Darol was when we would run up and down the bleachers at Santa Barbara City College. He was so strong and always down to work out. He also taught me how to drive. It was a scary experience, but he stuck with me and helped me to relax and drive without zigzagging through lanes on the freeway. He gave me life advice and became more than a friend who I could always rely on.

Janet was quiet but also very kind. She was very smart and seemed to have answers to everything. She was my 'google' for everything. I would reach out to Janet about anything related to my school, travelling in and out of America and so on. Janet also proofread my essay papers in high school and college. She was one of the reasons why I improved my English. Brian was my age and a soccer fanatic just like me. I didn't have half of Brian's academic brain though. Just like his parents, Brian was very knowledgeable and could hold any conversation. We had a lot in common when it came to sports and working out.

Before I came to America, I often thought American teenagers were lazy. I guess I developed that fallacy from the American movies I watched in Ghana. Most of the American teenagers appeared to whine about everything and very dependent on their parents.

'Look at them. A bunch of good-for-nothing whiners,' my Ghanaian friends would often refer to American teenagers as we watch American movies.

When I got to America, that was the notion that I had, but thankfully Brian changed that. I love to run; I can run for days. I developed that endurance from constantly running back and forth to some of the dirty beaches of Ghana. Most of my ignorant high school mates often teased that my ability to run for days came from my primitive life in Africa, running away from lions or chasing around impalas for dinner. I would often smile and correct them,

'No. Actually, there are cars in Ghana.' I didn't know Brian loved to run until we had to do a beep test for our Santa Barbara Soccer club team.

The beep test is a running test used to estimate our aerobic capacity. In the test, we have to run from one line to another before a timed beep. We continue running back and forth, each time reaching the line before the next beep. You run until you can't get to the line before the beep. Once you give up, the test is over, and the number of laps is recorded. As the test continues, the time between beeps gets shorter. The whole team was lined up and we heard the beep. We hit the ground running, going from one line to the other under the direction of the beep. We went from level one to level eight with no problem. Everyone was breathing hard and making it to the line. Level ten came, and half of the team gave up. The rest of us kept running. By level fifteen, it was just four of us left and then it came down to Brian and me. Level sixteen, level seventeen, level eighteen and we were still running. I was surprised to see him running with me. Why is he not out yet? I began to wonder whether Brian was an African in disguise. I was taking glances at him as I ran to see if he was going to give up. He just kept running, with a look of determination on his face.

At this point, our teammates were shivering, standing in the cold and looking to see which one of us would drop out. They started yelling at us to give up, so we could get to playing soccer. Brian and I both looked at each other at level twenty and as a truce, we both walked out together. That day was a big teaching moment for me. Don't judge a book by its cover. Brian and I became very close from then on. He became my 'brother from another mother'. We trained together, ran together and did a lot of things together besides schoolwork.

Then there was Katie, a very intelligent girl just like her parents. Katie was very outgoing and quite a popular girl for her love for people and openness to learn about different cultures and meet different people. Katie made me banana bread in high school and college. I loved her banana bread a lot and always looked forward to it. Katie also loved and played soccer. We would train with her sometimes. Katie would end up at Stanford University just like her mom and dad. Besides the Joseffs, I also had a few families that were more than friends to me.

These families were: the Foleys, the Camarenas the Csetes, the Sullivans, the Shwartz, the Carsons, the Johnstons, and the Neeleys. They all opened their homes to me and treated me as one of their own children. As a result of their loving care, the duffle bag that I brought to America turned into two new big suitcases filled with lots of clothes and shoes. Despite their love and care, I was never immune to the cultural shock and shame that came with going to a new place and learning a new culture.

One of the biggest cultural shocks in America was seeing so many young girls participate in organized youth soccer. As I mentioned earlier, traditional gender roles prevented most girls in Ghana from taking part in contact sports like soccer. Any girl who engaged in soccer was considered as unfeminine or a 'man-woman' for breaking gender roles. During my first week in America, I joined the Santa Barbara Soccer Club. At my first club practice at La Colina Junior High, I was very surprised to see two girls' teams practicing next to my team. One team was younger, perhaps they were about ten years old, and the other girls team looked like my age, around fifteen years old. I spent most of that practice looking at the girls than training with my team as if I had never seen white girls before in my life.

I was very happy to see that girls had equal opportunities to play sports here in America as compared to Ghana. My curiosity led me to set my eyes on one of the girls on the team that was the same age group as my team. I later found out that her name was Kaitlynn. I thought Kaitlynn was very beautiful but never had the courage to say 'hi' or introduce myself to her. Whenever my team was jogging around the field for warmups, and I made eye contact with Kaitlynn, I would immediately look away and my heart would be pounding as we jogged by where her team was sitting. I was shy I would say, but mostly because I was all business when I got to America. My goal was to get a better education and to play professional soccer. I didn't have time for any girl at the time. I had the same serious demeanor at soccer practice and in school. I barely spoke to girls at my school and gave the impression of being too serious with everything I did at school.

To be honest, I didn't speak very much, and it was hard for people here in America to understand my accent, so why make a fool out of myself by trying to talk to any girl, especially to Kaitlynn. But I never forgot about Kaitlynn though. I would usually stay to watch her games since we played for the same club and our home games were sometimes back-to-back with the girls' team games. Kaitlynn was tough on the field and I was drawn to her hard work as a defender. Thanks to social media, I was able to become friends with Kaitlynn, and finally had the courage to keep in touch with her.

I know you probably want to know what happened after that. Well, fast forward to January 2017, after improving on my accent and gaining more confidence, I was able to have the courage to ask Kaitlynn out. Indeed, it took me about ten years, but I did it, and we were engaged to be married in July 2019.

I experienced another cultural shock on my way to out of the airport to meet Debbie and the other Ghanaian boys picking me up at LAX. I overheard a heated conversation between an older lady and a small girl. The lady looked like she was in her forties while the girl projected an image of a fourteen-year-old girl. Looking at the facial resemblance, I concluded that they were related. This thought was confirmed when the little girl yelled out to her mom,

'Shut up, Mom.' Without understanding most of the words in the argument that ensued between them, I was surprised to see that the girl was talking back to her mother in a tone that was never tolerated in Ghana.

Within African families, an extremely high value is placed on respecting, obeying, and learning from your elders in the kinship network and community. When we fail to show respect to anyone older than us, we are punished for it. The whole time in my head, I was like,

'This girl is about to catch a whopping' from her mom, but the cane or whip or slap was never in sight.

Am I dreaming? Or am I watching a prank show? These thoughts ran through my mind and I was surprised that the little girl was still alive after talking back to her mom in a very disrespectful manner. Growing up in Ghana, you can hardly find any child arguing with their parents or anyone older than themselves in a disrespectful manner. Any child who does not do what they are told, when they are told to do it, is considered in society as a bad child or a child possessed by demons. In Ghana, this form of children respecting their parents projects a healthy awareness that children are subordinate to the parents so long as they live under their parents' roof; that the parents make all the final decisions in the home, and no backtalk or rude behavior is permitted.

When I saw the little girl back-talking to her mom at the airport, she appeared to have no respect for her parents. During my first week in America, I couldn't count the number of times I saw children talk back to their parents, saying the rudest things to their parents, claiming rights as though they were equal to their parents even though they were dependent on their parents for everything.

The experience brought many questions to my mind. Are children allowed to run wild in this country? Why were they not getting the beating that I was used to in Ghana? As I learned the American culture, I came to several conclusions in my mind. Unlike African children whose rights are overshadowed by the harsh reality of poverty, children in America have more rights and are highly protected by law. Also, unlike African children who are subordinate to everything their parents or any elder in society tells them, American children talk back to their parents to express their views on issues concerning them.

Other than the cultural shock, I faced several shameful moments that became a learning opportunity for me. The biggest challenge I faced in my first few days in America was the idea of choice. I never in my fifteen years in Ghana, had I ever thought that deciding what to eat could be so hard until I got to America. There were too many choices with everything, which gave me a lot of stress. Sometimes I felt it would be easier for me to not eat at all. At my home in Ghana, I ate whatever I was given. We didn't even have a dining table to sit down and eat at.

My grandmother would line up the food on the ground and we ate whatever was in the plastic bowl. On some occasions when we didn't have any money to eat, I went to bed on an empty stomach, so I didn't even have to look in the bowl to see what I had. Also, in the academy, I ate what was on the menu for us. We didn't have the choice to decide which food we were in the mood for at that time. The next morning, my host mom, Janet, was excited to feed me some breakfast. She asked if I wanted cereal or something else. Frankly, I just went with the first name she mentioned, and the rest sounded like gibberish to me. I had never had cereal before or at least didn't know what cereal was.

'I will like to have some cereal please,' I replied graciously.

Immediately after I said that she asked again, 'would you prefer to have cheerios, granola, fruity loop, or honey bunches of oats?'

Again, I had no idea what those were. I began to sweat a little bit and was going crazy trying to keep up with all the names for a bowl of cereal. I didn't even know how to pronounce half of those names.

'Yes, cheerios please,' I replied, again, the only name I remembered from the rest of the list.

As she started putting the cheerios in the bowl, she asked me if I wanted some milk. In Ghana, we put milk in hot chocolate, tea, coffee, rice water, and porridge. The milk we had in Ghana at the time was canned. The milk had a dark yellowish color to it when you pour it out of the can. It was thick and creamy and came in a variety of brands like Ideal Milk, Peak Milk, and Carnation Milk.

'Yes, I would have some milk, thank you,' I replied proudly thinking I was at least familiar with something.

To my surprise, she asked, 'what kind of milk do you like? 2%, fat-free, or whole milk?'

I began to sweat about it. What are all these different choices? I had never heard of the different choices of milk. I settled for 2% because it was very easy for me to remember and pronounce. My struggle to choose food did not end at Janet's house. Whenever we went to a restaurant, I would find it very hard to order from the menu. I would often just point at the picture that was drawn in the menu.

My nemesis of food choices was a restaurant where there were menus with no pictures in them. It affected my whole appetite, as I often found myself trying to figure out how to pronounce the names or what every word meant on the menu. I began to beat the system and came out with a 'genius' idea to solve my food choosing anxiety. Whenever we went to a restaurant, I would let my Ghanaian friend, Nana, go first, and then I would just say to the waiter/waitress, 'same,' gesturing to what Nana got. I ate the same food as Nana would order even when it was too spicy, cheesy, or chewy. One day though, I faced my worst fear at a local Mexican restaurant by the University of California, Santa Barbara (UCSB) campus.

When we got to the Mexican restaurant, Nana ordered first as usual. I was caught up talking to someone behind me, so I didn't catch what Nana ordered. When it was time for me to order, I just said, 'same.'

The waiter became a little confused. 'Sir, I'm afraid we don't have "same" on the menu,' he replied with a faint smile.

Nana overheard the conversation and he came by and told the waiter that what I meant to say was that I wanted exactly what he ordered. I was often teased for saying, 'same' all the time, but I knew it was the best way to save myself from the headache of choosing what to eat as I learned to adapt to the American culture.

Struggling with choosing the kind of food I wanted to eat was just one problem I faced as I figured out how to keep up with the American accent and speak better English. American English sounded too fast for me and the crazy part was that people would have no idea what I was saying to them when I had conversations with them. They still don't understand what I say now, but at least I'm aware of it. I would be holding conversations with people and all they would say was 'yes' at the end of everything I was saying. I could tell from their faces that it sounded like gibberish to them because they would just laugh randomly in parts of the conversations that were clearly not funny. I remember one time I was telling someone about my family and how I came to America alone.

When I reached the part where I was talking about the death of my grandfather, they said 'yes!' from nowhere and started laughing. I was taken aback, but I concluded that they clearly had no idea what I was saying. The first months in America were hard, especially when I talked in my thick African accent. During my first week at Dunn School, we had our new students' orientation to get to know the faculty and staff of the school. We were in a circle and we had to go around and tell everyone about our name, where we come from, and our favorite food. I was in stress mode as I heard the assignment.

One by one, each student responded to the questions, which was often ended with a clap from everyone. When it was getting to my turn, I didn't know what to say as my favorite food. I knew people would not know my second favorite Ghanaian food, which is fufu and palm nut soup, which is prepared with cassava dough (this is made with palm nut cream, smoked fish, tomatoes, onions, minced garlic, black pepper, chili powder, salt, spices (magi), onion, water, cassava and plantains). I also didn't know the American food, and 'same' was not on the menu so I was screwed. I was panicking as it got to the next person before me.

The person started talking in the fast America accent, which was very difficult for me to keep up with but towards the end of mentioning his favorite food, I heard 'orange juice.' That was the only thing I picked up from his whole rant about himself. I knew what an orange was since I'd had oranges many times in Ghana and so I was happy I caught that part.

When it got to my turn, I nervously cleared my throat and said, 'My name is Kingsley, or you can call me Fifi. I'm from Ghana and my favorite food is...' My mind went blank as I was caught between saying fufu and palm nut soup or 'same.' I quickly remembered 'orange juice' from the previous person. 'Oh, my favorite food is orange juice,' I replied with a look of confidence and cool on my face. The teacher sat there for a second without rallying everyone to clap for me.

He said to me, 'your favorite food is orange juice huh?'

I replied boldly, 'Yes I love it.'

Again, he paused for a second and said, 'interesting, you really love your orange juice.'

I nodded in reply. A few seats away from me, I saw one guy gesturing to his friend about the motions of chewing orange juice.

He murmured to his friend, 'wait, how do you even chew orange juice?'

His friend just shrugged, and sharply said, 'I know, it's crazy.' They all finally clapped for me, but it was such a different clap compared to what everyone got before me, it was an awkward clap.

I sat there with a look of embarrassment. I learned an important lesson: never copy what people are doing just to fit in or to look cool. Always, stay true to yourself, stay humble and work hard. Another pivotal incident was when we were doing a popcorn reading in our English class (a popcorn reading is when students are randomly called on to read aloud to the whole class). When it got to my turn, everyone was flipping their pages trying to figure out which page I was trying to read from. The room went silent after I finished reading and everyone had a look of confusion on their face.

In order to diffuse the awkwardness, the teacher said, 'Thank you for reading, Kingsley. Now can we have someone read from where Kingsley left off?'

The next person to read asked, 'Which paragraph should I read?'

The teacher was trying so hard to be nice to me and didn't know what to reply to the student. Finally, after regaining her train of thought, she replied, 'Just start from the top,' avoiding any awkward eye contact with me.

Once again, I saw one of the students whisper to his friend, 'Hey it's the orange juice guy.' His friend turned around to get a good look at me. He quickly turned around as he locked eyes with me. I could tell he was giggling, trying so hard to prevent himself from laughing out loud.

'Yes, you're right, it's him,' he whispered to his friend with a big smile on his face.

It was a very embarrassing few months, as I became the 'orange juice guy' and 'same,' but I did not lose hope. From that moment on, I knew I had to work extra hard to improve my English and to get better grades. I took advantage of every minute to read and asked a lot of questions in class. Whenever we had to write any research paper, I made sure I let as many people proofread it before I turned it in, which meant that I had to write the papers way in advance before the due date.

Despite being teased by my friends, I went on to get straight A's and finished the school year with a 4.0 GPA, making me the first Right to Dream graduate to receive an academic excellence award. Right to Dream had given me the opportunity for a better life and I knew I had to work hard to make my dreams come true in America.

Growing up in Ghana, my grandfather always used to tell me that, 'Yehowa shira nea oboa neho,' which translated to, 'God blesses those who help themselves.' Those words became my talisman in all aspects of my life. As a firm believer in hard work, I strongly believed that when you live your dream through your hard work, success will follow everywhere you go. I never lost hope because I believed that if I work hard, then my hope for a better life will be stronger and my dreams will come true. My success in the classroom and off the soccer field of Dunn School earned me a scholarship to the University of California, Santa Barbara.

CHAPTER 11

Dream fulfilled

The biggest adventure you can take is to live the life of your dreams—
Oprah Winfrey

The transition from high school to college was a very interesting process for me. I was very privileged to receive several full-scholarship offers from various prestigious institutions including Harvard, Yale, University of California, Los Angeles (UCLA), Stanford, University of California, Santa Barbara (UCSB), Duke, and Michigan. I put these names here not to blow my own horn but to show how hard work and the desire to focus on your dreams can lead you to opening new doors of opportunity.

After several days researching and many discussions about the different schools, I decided to go to UCSB. This was not because of its famous characteristic as a 'party school.' Although partying sounded fun, I was more into achieving my goals because of where I came from and the responsibility that rested on my shoulders to support my family back home.

I came to America to achieve a quality education and to play professional soccer. I can't count the number of times I thought about those words. UCSB appealed to me because they had a great soccer program and a great education system. I saw UCSB as the best opportunity to achieve my dream. Did I mention that I also had some Ghanaian friends like Waid Ibrahim and Michael Tetteh who were already student-athletes at UCSB?

I felt that being in the same school as them would help me to settle into the school quickly. I moved into an apartment complex on the UCSB campus called Garden Court to embark on my college journey at UCSB. I would be sharing the two-bedroom apartment with three other teammates on the soccer team. My roommates would be David Opoku, a tall forward who from Ghana as well. Then we had Eric Reyes, a goalkeeper native of Miami and then Ray Ezra Zimbwa, a strong midfielder who originated from Uganda. Ray quickly adopted the nickname, 'situation' for his love of impersonating the American reality show, Jersey Shore, that ran from 2009 through 2012.

The four of us developed a strong relationship, often teasing each other and enjoying our first year of our college experience. We established a system where we contributed to purchase groceries together in bulk and we also shared the household chores. Our first year as roommates was good together until Eric Reyes transferred to FIU and David Opoku left to play professional soccer in Europe. Ray and I would be the last people standing until we would part ways after college.

My host dad, Darol, helped me to move, carrying two suitcases containing all my clothes and shoes. My host mom, Janet, had two grocery bags full of food from the grocery store. They had a look of excitement on their faces as they helped me to unpack my luggage in the dresser. They constantly reminded me how much they loved me and how proud they were of me.

It felt like I was in the movie, The Blind Side except I would be playing soccer instead of football and I got into UCSB mainly because of a combination of both my academic and soccer prowess. I couldn't tell whether they were happy because I got into UCSB or whether they were relieved that I was finally out of the house and 'on my own.'

I believe the reason was the former because they always extended an invitation for me to come to their house for dinner and to stay with them whenever we were on break. Nevertheless, a few days after I moved into my apartment at UCSB, I set a goal for myself. I wrote that goal in my heart and in my mind to graduate with a degree and to play in Major League Soccer. Every day for me was about hard work and making sure I remained focused to achieve that goal. My hard work was about improving on the soccer skills and making sure I excelled in the classroom as well.

I quickly learned on the soccer field that the college style of soccer was more physical and direct than I anticipated. In the Right to Dream Academy, everything was about technical ability and understanding of the game. I was able to stand out because of my ability to read the game and movement of the ball. That was not the case for my first few days playing in college. Most of the players we played against were twice my size and just wanted to play long balls over the top. I was having difficulty adapting to the college style of soccer at the beginning because they quickly pushed me off the ball like a fly.

The long balls they constantly played over the top played to their strength and physicality because they easily out jumped me to head the ball above my five-foot eight-inch short frame. I remember we were playing the Mexican U23 National team in an exhibition and I looked like a little kid in the game. I was able to pass but was dispossessed or had the ball taken away from me on many occasions as the other players used their strength.

I felt lost in the game and I was just running around like a little fly, not strong enough to absorb the physicality of the opponent. After that game, I knew I needed to work especially if I wanted to play soccer at the professional level. I needed to go to the gym for strength training. I had to also change my eating habits to help me to get stronger. During that time, I was privileged to work with one of the world-renowned strength and conditioning facility called P3—Peak, Performance, Project[iv] .

I met with Dr Marcus Elliot, who was a very nice guy, and talked about what I needed to work on and my goal of playing professional soccer after college. He readily agreed to help me and together with his great team including Sam, Arie and others, they were able to design a program for me to improve my strength. I did a lot of work with P3 to help me to get stronger and compete with those big guys on the field. Meanwhile, I was without a doubt one of the most technical players on the team. I was able to pass the ball with much more ease and adroitness that came from experience from playing at the Right to Dream Academy, at Fulham Academy, and at Dunn School.

With no surprise, I also established myself as one of the players who could run for days on the team. I was head to head with another UCSB player from Nigeria, Machael David, who had the heart and endurance of a marathon runner. Machael David and I had a lot of fun outpacing our teammates during our long-distance pre-season training. It looked like we had the same endurance level as we went head to head on any fitness drills. Macheal David would often joke in his African broken English accent,

'Oga, make u give up naa…Eii Ghana man,' which directly translates as, 'just give up bro.'

I would often laugh as we raced around the field. We would run until we were told not to run anymore. We would always go head to head to see who had the most endurance. The beep test was too easy for us, and playing a full ninety-minute game became like a warmup for us. We finished our UCSB careers in a tie for the most fit soccer athlete during our time there.

Meanwhile, I also faced some challenges in the classroom at UCSB. Although I was a good student, I was having a hard time with big lecture classes at UCSB. In high school at Dunn, my class sizes were around eight to twelve students in a class at a time which allowed for great face to face interaction and discussions with teachers and peers.

I remember I walked into my first class at UCSB at IV theatre, an auditorium that housed over a hundred students at a time. At the beginning I had a hard time taking notes. The professors moved fast through the curriculum and didn't waste time answering lots of questions. I didn't know what to write and I was often behind writing the important points down from lectures. As I busily tried to take notes in my lectures, the next thing I realized, the quarter was almost close to an end with mid-terms and finals. Other than the small class sizes, Dunn school was also on a semester system which meant that I had a lot of time before and in between mid-term exams.

Everything in the classroom at UCSB went too fast. Lectures and finals came as if they only had one day apart. I remember I got a C in my first exams. It was an economics class. I loved economics, but the lectures were just too fast for me to keep up. Receiving my first C grade came as a shock to me. I cried that day and vowed to never receive such a grade again. I knew I had to do a lot of reading and research to keep up.

As time progressed, I began to adapt. I noticed that I didn't have to write everything during lectures, but I had to pay attention to the key points and how they related to the class theme and objective. I also continued to ask lots of questions in class, among my peers and utilized 'office hours' discussions with professors to learn and to ask questions about the course. Despite my slow start, my determination to improve in the classroom and on the soccer field began to pay off. I slowly began to establish myself as a starter on the soccer field, thanks to Marcus and the staff at P3. By the time I reached my junior year of college, my name had appeared in many newspaper articles in Santa Barbara, and I had gained attention from most of the coaches at Major League Soccer. After my sophomore year, Michael Tetteh was drafted by the Seattle Sounders in Major League Soccer to pursue his professional career. He left college without completing his degree. By the time I reached the end of my junior year of college, my roommate, David Opoku, had also left college to play professional soccer in Europe, again without graduating.

Towards the end of my junior year in college, I decided to obtain a college degree before leaving to pursue playing professional soccer. I wanted to graduate in three years instead of the traditional four years. I met with our academic advisor at the time, Kelly Barsky, to develop a plan towards making that happen. It was one of the most intense few months of college. I was taking five to six classes of twenty-one units at a time, a workload that is doable for regular students but very difficult for a division one college athlete.

I was determined and I believed that I could get it done. I limited my time of going out to parties and dedicated the time doing my homework. The most difficult times came when we travelled to away soccer games and I had to do my homework on the bus. At this point, I was training very hard and my social life turned to doing homework.

I remember one time we were coming from a game at UC Davis, about a five-hour journey from UCSB. We won the game, and on our way back, I looked up and saw all my teammates sleeping in their seats. I was still up reading a book and started on a paper that was due the next day. The most I slept at night during that period was about four hours. I was always reading or writing a research paper or training to improve on my soccer skills. Sometimes I felt physically exhausted and mentally drained, but I kept pressing on.

My teammates often teased me to 'get a life' or stop being boring and live a little. Indeed, there is a time for everything but for me, everything is about sacrifice. I tended to smile and laugh a lot because it eased the responsibility I was carrying on my shoulders. The smile hid the suffocation and pain that I went through. I am who I am because of the values and standards I set for myself. My life was boring, yes, but I was determined to make my dream a reality.

In order to receive my diploma by the end of November 2013, I had to 'walk' early or in other words 'graduate early' before completing all the units to receive my diploma. As I wore my black gown and black cap for 'graduation' listening to the graduation speech with a smile, I realized that I was almost there and needed to give my last push to achieve that goal.

By the end of December 2013, I had finished all the required units to obtain my diploma. I got the school part down, now I was faced with everything on the soccer field. My last year on the soccer team started slowly. I started to feel pain around my groin. Throughout my sophomore and junior year, I received a lot of cortisone shots in my groin to mask the pain to continue to play. By the time I reached my senior year, both sides of my groin were in constant pain.

The best way for groin problems to heal is to take time and rest. Unfortunately, I had no time on my side to take off and besides my team needed me in that central mid-field. I started the first three games of my senior year of college nursing my groin injury.

'This can't be,' I thought to myself. After all the hard work, I was not ready to hit a brick wall at the most important part of my college soccer career.

I was ready to persevere despite the pain. My injury was getting worse and the regular season was about to begin. I missed the first few exhibition games through the groin injury. I watched on the sidelines as my teammates battled on the field without me. Those would be the first few games I missed in my entire professional soccer career. After several physical therapy treatments and cortisone injections, I was back on my feet again.

My first game back from injury, I started off the bench. We were playing Fullerton, a team known for its physicality. It felt weird starting off the bench, but it was better to slowly ease my way into the game instead of rushing to get injured again. As much as I hated sitting on the bench, I was ready to get back on the field. I remember sitting on the bench and thinking what I needed to do when I got the opportunity to get on the field. They played the whole first half without me.

We were winning two-nil at the end of the first half, and perhaps my coach, Tim Vom Steeg, didn't seem to need me on the field. The second half started with the same casual intensity. They matched us physically, but we were technically better. As the second half was heading to a stalemate after twenty-five minutes of battle, I was instructed to warm up. After five minutes of warmup, Tim instructed me to go on to the right side of the field.

What does this mean? I thought. Have been axed from my usual position from central mid-field? I was starting to get nervous and thought that I lost my starting position on the team.

I was nevertheless happy to get back on the field after a long absence. I went on the field and connected my first pass. It was a forward pass to our forward, Achille Campeon, a strong six-foot forward from France. I was doing everything as simple as possible by making sure I completed all my passes. My groin seemed to be holding steadily after several sprints to chase after their left full back. I got another ball and gave a pass to our midfielder, Adam Staferstein, a very technical and humble midfielder who grew to be one of my best friends on the team.

When Adam received the ball, he switched it to the left side to Drew Murphy, a left-footed player whose crosses are excellently placed like the famous David Beckham. As soon as Drew received the ball, I saw that he put his head down to serve a cross to the box. I ran as quickly as possible to the box and to my surprise, I outjumped their left full back and headed the ball to the net. I couldn't believe I scored. I rarely scored for UCSB as I played a more defensive role in mid-field for the team.

My goal brought a measure of a standing ovation from the whole crowd in the stadium as if to welcome me back from injury. As I made my way to the corner flag to celebrate my goal, I joyfully made the robot movement dance which I promised two of the staff members at UCSB athletics, Kayla Smith and Christina Baglas, that I would do. Both Kayla and Christina became some of my all-time favorite members of the staff at UCSB for their constant support of my dreams and their encouragement.

My celebration was far off from robot dance moves but at least I tried and dedicated it to them to show appreciation for everything they continued to do for me. As my teammates came to congratulate me and enjoy the moment with me, I felt a sense of breakthrough in my heart. That goal brought a renewed sense of confidence. From that day, the rest of the games for the season saw me back to my starting role in central mid-field. I played a significant role to help UCSB win the conference and book our place in the national tournament.

Despite all the highs and lows, my last game for UCSB ended with a red card that was shown to me in the first two minutes into the game. It was our first game of the NCAA tournament against Penn State. I went throughout my college career without receiving a yellow card, but I ended with a red card. When you are shown a yellow card, you still get a second chance to keep playing, but being shown a red card meant that you are ejected from the game at that time you received the card.

I was flying high with confidence. I was playing well at the time and believed that my team was the favorite to win that game. The game started in a quiet fashion, as the opposing team seemed to be nervous from the roaring noise of our supporters. I received a ball from the left side of the field and switched it to the right side of the field. Our right back attempted a pass to our forward which was intercepted, causing the ball to land between me and one of their midfielders. As I was sprinting to get the ball, I calculated that I wouldn't get there before he would, and so I did a slide tackle to sweep the ball with my extended foot as I landed on the side of my body. The next thing I saw, the opposing player jumped and made a loud noise as if I had injured him in the process.

Without clear assessment, the referee immediately showed me a red card. My teammates and I wanted to protest but was to no avail. I walked straight to the locker room for an early shower as I listened to the game from the empty locker room. We ended up losing the game one-nil. I was very sad and felt a sense of letting my team down. It was a very emotional moment as I witnessed my team lose out on the NCAA tournament from my only rushed tackle. I went to bed that night without eating. I was just devastated and with mixed feelings about my goal of playing professional soccer.

I thought to myself, does this mean that my dream of playing professional soccer is over? One red card and I'm done? What do I do next? As I grappled with these questions throughout the night, I dozed off with sadness in my heart and held tight onto the hope I still had.

The next morning, I issued a statement on my social media page expressing how sorry I was about letting my team down, which generated a lot of 'likes' and comments from friends and family who encouraged me to press on. I was determined to work even harder towards my dream. The next day, I went to the gym, did a workout and pictured myself playing professional soccer somewhere. I continued to train with high hopes.

Two weeks after the red card incident, I was invited to be part of the 2014 Major League Soccer Combine which was given to the top fifty men's college players in the country.

I was the only player from UCSB that was invited to the combine which was held in Tampa, Florida. The combine was like a tryout, something I had been familiar with at Right to Dream and Fulham. The combine lasted for five days and I had the opportunity to play with and against some of the top athletes in the country. I also had the opportunity to talk to MLS coaches who expressed their interest in my play. The combine was intense. We were tested for speed, vertical jump, and soccer skills on the field. I did the best I could and left the rest to God.

On January 22, 2014, I was drafted by Columbus Crew in the Major League Soccer Super Draft, and it was a crowning moment after years of hard work and determination. I became the second Right to Dream graduate to sign for an MLS side, following in the footsteps of Michael Tetteh, who had signed with the Seattle Sounders two years earlier. I officially signed my first professional contract with Columbus Crew on February 14, 2014 after a good pre-season. As I put the pen on paper to sign my contract, I was filled with tears of joy. I began to wonder how happy the seven-year-old Fifi or my grandfather would be, seeing me sign that piece of paper to start my professional career. It was a great feeling of finally achieving the success I had only once hoped for. The Dream fulfilled at last!

CHAPTER 12

Fifi Soccer Foundation

Where there is no vision, there is no hope—George Washington Carver

The one thing that connected me to my past was giving back and helping others in need. Something about the way people treated me ever since I came to the US stuck with me. The time that people put into me is the reason that I am who I am today. My mind has always been swimming with ideas about giving back and my heart has been bursting with a yearning desire to help others.

I had a deep desire to give back because people had believed in me and that helped me to hold onto my ray of hope for the future. I wanted to do for others what others had done for me. Giving kids hope and determination so that they have a chance in the future. The moments I spent improving someone's life—whether holding the door for them or lending a helping hand to older ones as they go down the stairs— kept me in high spirits. Looking back at my childhood, I believe that children are the future.

I'd always loved working with children. I suppose it was in my blood. I had fond memories of playing soccer with children. Most of my friends often teased me for acting like a child every time they wanted to pick on me. I would often be seen walking or playing with children in my neighborhood. Sometimes they would get me in trouble with their fake tears when I unintentionally kicked the ball at them, and it hit them in the face. But time and again, after verbal abuse from their parents, I would be back again playing with them.

I guess I have always been fascinated about the way children act with a lot of imagination, carefree spirits and the willingness to learn about everything with their overly used word, 'why,' after every response you give them. Most importantly, I strongly believe that children are the best agents for change. Children are the future of the world.

One of the most powerful tools of humanity is love. We love because we care about people and we want to do everything in our power to make them happy. We give money to charity because we want to bring about change in our society. Yet, somewhere along the way, we lost the motive behind our giving. We went from giving out of love to giving out our surplus. As Stephen Patela[v] explains in his TEDx Talk, 'Philanthropy is not about how much money we have but about one who loves and serves mankind.'

The reality of our giving has impacted the harsh reality of the world. While one half of the world enjoys over-abundance, the other half lives in the dark shadows of poverty. When we start caring about what is going on in the world, we are moved to action. If we all have a yearning desire to love mankind, together we can solve the problems of humanity.

Towards the middle of my first year with Columbus Crew, I had to have hip surgery, which brought an end to my professional soccer. It was a devastating experience, as I had to take a whole year to do physical therapy to heal. It was a very arduous period, but it helped me to change the way I perceived the world. As I went through everyday recuperating, I began to think about the bigger picture.

My childhood dream had always been to play professional soccer, but I reshaped my thought to feel the pain that people go through, especially young children in underprivileged countries like Ghana. At this point, my hope for the future had changed. I was no longer dedicating my life to become a professional soccer player, but I realized that I was conditioning my heart to make the most impact in the world.

In 2016, after I resolved in my heart to 'hang up my soccer cleats,' I turned my attention to coaching. I became a coach at Santa Barbara Soccer Club. I have been with the club for about four years now. Being a mentor to the children and teaching them to be better citizens of the world brings a lot of satisfaction in coaching. As a coach, I work on developing the soccer skills of the children I work with. Seeing them light up when they finally do what I instruct them to do on the field brings me a lot of joy. My ultimate goal is to inspire them, to give them a purpose, and to help them to develop a good heart and mind to tackle the problems of the world in the future.

As I continue to work hard to be a better coach and role model to these children, my desire to make an impact extends beyond the soccer field of Santa Barbara Soccer Club.

On June 29 2018, the Santa Barbara newspaper[vi] reported:

Fifi Baiden is a success story but now he is giving back to make sure others can achieve great feats. The former UCSB soccer star has his own foundation in his home country of Ghana called Fifi Soccer Foundation. The foundation provides children housing, food and education. Baiden is hoping to work with companies in Ghana to eventually find these kids internships and jobs so that they can achieve success in Ghana without having to leave the country. Baiden was selected into the Right to Dream Academy which eventually placed him at Dunn High School in Los Olivos where he earned a scholarship to play soccer at UCSB. He excelled on the field and in the classroom for the Gauchos. Baiden was drafted by Major League Soccer's Columbus Crew in 2014 but an injury cut his pro soccer career short. Now his goal is to help children, particularly orphans.

From my humble beginnings, to the rise in the USA, I have always had the desire to help people, especially children. It breaks my heart to see all the pain and suffering in this world. After everything that I went through, I want to do my best to be a part of the movement to bring an end to human suffering. My heart beats very fast whenever I see the pictures of hungry faces of children. It moves me to do something in order to bring about change. I guess I don't want people to go through the suffering I went through growing up. Like we all do, I want people to be happy. I want to see the smiles on their faces when they wake up to life every day.

Change is prevalent when every single organism on this earth decides to take action. When I was at the Right to Dream Academy, I used to give part of my dinner to some of the younger players whenever they complained of being hungry after eating their food. I would also help them with their homework and even teach them how to read and write in English. I morphed into a leader through my actions. I have a quiet personality and am never the outspoken person in the room, but I believe in being a leader by serving the needs of others. In his book, The Servant as Leader, Greenleaf[vii] (1970) explained that:

'The servant-leader is servant first. It begins with the natural feeling that one wants to serve first.'

My yearning desire to give back and serve others in the same way I've been blessed moved me to action. I want to lead by being a servant first.

Back in July 2013, during my junior year of college, I volunteered at the non-government organization, Orphan Aid Africa, which aimed to provide a better life to orphans and the poor children of Ghana. I was saddened to see so many underprivileged children wandering the streets of Ghana with so much time on their hands and no future. Talking to some of these street children, I learned that many of them came from broken homes and were abandoned by their families due to economic hardship. As a result of poverty, these children were driven onto the streets to fend for themselves, begging, and stealing food.

In 2017, I was moved to start the Fifi Soccer Foundation to give hope and a better future to orphans and the poor children of Ghana. Each of our beneficiaries will receive a full scholarship from our program. It was a big task I took upon myself. There are so many missing pieces to put together to make it work. First, you need the vision, then you need the money, then the staff, then the children, and then the necessary equipment.

I started generating some support for the foundation by selling Fifi Soccer t-shirts online. I was surprised about how much support I got from the t-shirt. That gave me a lot of confidence to know that I was heading in the right direction. Then I knew I needed to get the capital to hire the staff and rent a place for the children to live. I spoke with a couple of generous donors that I knew—the Carsons, the Schulhofs, the Johstons, the Burnzs, and the Huiners and then I did a fundraiser as well.

Through generous donations, I was able to generate enough money to start the foundation. Now, we have about twenty beneficiaries and we provide them with education, food, clothing, shelter, and sports training to equip them with the necessary tools to succeed in life. We also have about ten staff members who work tirelessly to provide the best opportunity for the children. Fifi Soccer Foundation is designed to nurture and bring out the leadership in children, no matter their circumstances. We provide underprivileged Ghanaian children the opportunity to fulfil their potential and the capacity to elevate themselves, so they can help their families, their communities and their country. It starts with the children.

I was managing all the ins and outs of the foundation from the US; I had the staff, the children and generous contributors from the Santa Barbara Community. I was very happy to see so many people support my vision. However, it was very difficult for me to manage everything from such a great distance. I tried to Facetime with the staff and the children and constantly remind them of the vision of the foundation.

'We all have a role in making this work. We have the heart. Now, let us put in the work,' I would constantly tell them whenever I had the privilege to talk to them.

In the summer of 2018, I went to Ghana to visit my family and to see the foundation. It was the first time meeting the children and staff in person. It also had been five years since I last saw my family. It was both a special and educational moment for me. The last memory I had from Ghana was when my mom and Uncle Richard accompanied me to the airport at the Kotoka International Airport, a two-hour journey away from Abossey Okai.

They took turns kissing and hugging me as I said my final goodbyes. My mom was in tears, and constantly reminded me to take very good care of myself, and that she will keep me in prayers. Other than the airport memory of my mom and Uncle Richard, my memory of Ghana consisted of the poor economy; bad roads; the searing heat; the sticky dirt; plastic waste problem; mosquito bites; and happy black faces working their way in the blazing heat to make ends meet. Above all, there were no showers. Bathing was still primitive, consisting of putting water in a bucket and pouring it over yourself.

Five years separated my last encounter, and now I was going back to Ghana. I was ready to see the same Ghana I knew when I last left. When I got to the airport, I was taken aback by the improved and remodeled Kotoka International Airport, which looked like the busy airport in Chicago. I saw a few people charging their phones and using laptops as they waited for their flight. I was so confused.

As I made my way out of the airport, I was welcomed by the blazing heat. Indeed, some things can never change. The blazing heat certainly never changed. The sight of my Uncle Evans at the airport reminded me that 'I'm home.' We got into the taxi that was waiting with him. 'Watch out! Watch Out!' I said, alarm rising in my voice as the driver barely missed a food vendor on the left. Then I realized that he had swerved to avoid the motorist careening down the street on our right. Each time we nearly scraped another vehicle, I let out a little yelp. The driver and my Uncle Evans calmly sat there. There were four similar near-misses before we reached the first traffic light, at which point there were about five more because I forgot that none of the cars, trucks, bicyclists, pedestrians, or various animals follow the traffic signal in Ghana. After a few heart pounding incidents, I decided my best strategy was to try to ignore the road and concentrate on the tall and big buildings on the side of the roads as we drove by. I was so impressed by their great architectural designs.

'Those building were not there when I last left, right?' I asked my Uncle Evans as I pointed to the buildings through the buildings.

'They were built not too long ago,' he replied with a smile on his face.

As I gazed through the window and noticed all the big buildings, I was also surprised to see Range Rovers and BMWs driving by our taxi. The Ghana I remembered had changed drastically, I thought to myself. I thought the country was poor? I asked my uncle again, drawing his attention to the nice cars that drove next to us.

'The rich keep getting richer, and the poor keep getting poorer,' he replied with a sense of sadness in his tone.

After half an hour of driving, I was embarrassed by my behavior in the car, but most of all I was angry at the misinformation I had received about Ghana or Africa in general from the American media. After all, it was America that had seduced me into adopting its great culture and enjoying the opportunity it offered to me through its quality education and high standard of living. Ghana had truly changed since the last time I lived there.

The extended family looked to be getting bigger with more cousins and nieces. My mom was living with my grandmother as well as my younger brother, Samuel. They were overjoyed to see me. My mom was in tears of joy and my grandmother would not stop hugging and kissing me. After a few days, I visited all my uncles and aunts and expressed how shocked I was with the state of the country. They all agreed that the country had changed since the last time I left.

Somehow amid the chaos and poverty, most teenagers and adults still managed to have internet access on their phones. Social media was no longer a thing of the developed west, but a norm in the Ghanaian culture as well. Did you bring some iPhone? I need an iPad. Can you buy me a laptop? These were among the many requests from my friends and family when I began to settle in. These people had no money for food or money to buy data on their phone, and yet they wanted a technology that would keep them on social media.

What happened to money to buy food to eat? I thought to myself. Their relentless requests for technology goes to show the rapid growth of technology in developing countries like Ghana. It also shows that Ghanaians want to keep pace and connected with the rest of the developed world. After a few days of getting used to the country and spending time with the family, I went to my foundation to meet with the children and staff. I became very emotional to see the progress we'd made in the first year. Seeing the smiling faces of the children really brought joy to my heart, a feeling I will never forget. It is my hope that Fifi Soccer Foundation offers the tools for children to make a difference and give them opportunities for the future. Fifi Soccer Foundation is on the rise, and I pray that we will continue to touch the lives of many children. Looking back at the prophecy about my future, it makes me wonder whether it was exactly how my life turned out. Whether it's true or not, my mother's strong conviction about the prophecy is a big boost in my confidence in the truthfulness of that prophecy. I do believe in the prophecy, and I hope that it extends to impact the lives of others.

Epilogue

Optimism is the faith that leads to achievement. Nothing can be done without hope—Helen Keller

Why is Ghana so poor? Is it true that nothing good comes out of Africa? Is the curse of Ham really about Africans? Is that why we are dark-skinned compared to the rest of the world? These are among many thoughts from my early childhood. All you hear on the radio and see on the TV are the dying and starving children of Africa. Many religious people attribute the problems of Africa—diseases, deaths, stunted growth, and poverty—to the curse of Ham in the Bible.

In Genesis 9 of the Bible, we see how God blessed Noah and his sons Shem, Ham, and Japheth after the flood, reiterating the blessing given in Eden to Adam and Eve to be fruitful and multiply. However, one evening, Noah got drunk enjoying the fruits of his labor and lay uncovered in his tent. His son Ham, the father of Canaan, saw the nakedness of his father and told his brothers, who respectfully covered their father.

When Noah woke up from his stupor, he condemned Ham's bad behavior, saying, 'Cursed be Canaan; a servant of servants shall he be to his brothers.' As history demonstrated, Canaan's descendants migrated to settle in Africa. This led to the many misinterpretations that Africans are a cursed race, leading to the heinous crimes of genocide and slavery. Whether this curse is about Africa or not, the whole continent is plagued with poverty, leading to the rise of corruption in all aspect of society

As I got older and more educated, I realized that the problem is not in our blood or because of our dark skin or a curse from the Bible. I began to rationalize that most people live a better life because of their wealth. How do they get wealth? By having a better job. Who creates jobs? Well, businesses do. Interestingly, if you look at the most attractive destinations for investors to do business, African countries are less desirable because of its reputation for corruption or '419,' cunningly named after the article numbered 419 in the Nigerian Criminal Code, which deals with fraud.[viii] However, people become corrupt because of the lack of jobs available for them to accumulate wealth and to live a better life. Until we create more jobs, then the problems of Africa or other impoverished countries will continue to grow.

Indeed, African nations should come together and work together to create more job opportunities for its populations. I believe that when jobs are created, poverty rate will reduce, and this will help eliminate 419 from the continent. This will not only win the trust of foreign investors but will also bring hope to the future of Africa.

Prevention researchers[ix] have discovered that there are human strengths that act as buffers against human suffering: hope is one of them.

Shelley Taylor[x] and her collaborators argued that the positive effects of hope are mediated mainly at a cognitive level. An optimistic patient is more likely to practice habits that enhance health and to enlist social support. One of the most interesting sets of studies they discuss is the one that shows that persons high in optimism and hope are more likely to provide themselves with unfavorable information about their disease, thereby being better prepared to face up to the realities.

Our hope for the future helps us to overcome life crisis. When we change our attitude and mindset about ourselves, we will be able to persevere and transform our circumstances for the better. Never lose hope! Always focus on the positive aspect of life. Like the fish who is unaware of the water in which it swims, people often take for granted a certain amount of hope. But hope is a very important condition that allows us to go on living. If we believe in hope, any number of objective obstacles in our lives can be faced with equanimity and even joy.

On May 23 2014, I was sitting in my little apartment in Columbus Ohio after I got back from training. My phone rang three times and as I was about to get it, I saw that I had received several text messages from friends and family. What is going? Is everything okay? These were among the many thoughts ran through my mind as I checked the first message. The first message was from one of my former UCSB teammates, and it read: Hey bro, how are you? Did you hear about the mass shooting in Isla Vista? The words of a mass shooting happening at UCSB, a school so dear to my heart, got my heart racing. I immediately went online and googled, 'mass shooting in Isla Vista'. I was shaking at this point as I read the story: twenty-two-year-old Elliot Rodger killed six people and injured fourteen others near the campus of University of California, Santa Barbara, before killing himself inside his vehicle. I was flabbergasted and appalled about a person committing such a heinous crime against humanity. I have heard of mass shootings before, but this just hit home. I quickly called most of my friends and family that were in Santa Barbara to make sure they were doing okay.

From their tone of voice, I could tell the whole community was in agony, grieving the death of loved ones. Over the course of the years, over 1,000 people have been killed through mass shootings, the recent of this was in Thousand Oaks, California where twelve people were killed at a country music dance hall. There had been many heartbreaking reports of mass shootings in schools, churches, clubs etc. but one thing that always stood out to me despite these tragic moments was how the community came together.

As politicians debate about gun violence and gun control, we hear words with hashtags like #IslaVistaStrong, #ThousandOaksStrong etc. to represent the strength and unity of humanity. In the face of tragedy, the community did not lose hope in humanity. Hope is the only thing that kept them going and made them believe that there is some good in this world. We live in a world where wars, poverty, and mass shootings have become the norm in society. No matter what our circumstance, there is always something better to look forward to in life.

During her appearance on the chat show Ellen in February 2018, the former First Lady, Michelle Obama, said, 'We show empathy, we care for each other, you know, we do have a lot in common. That's what it means to lead with hope and that's all we have, is hope.' Genuine hope is like a bright torchlight that helps us to see beyond our present trials and to face the future with courage and joy.

This word, hope, is also an essential element of faith in all religions today. The Bible defines faith as 'the assured expectation of things hoped for...' (Hebrews 11: 1). In fact, the words 'hope,' 'hoped,' and 'hoping,' appear over 160 times in the Bible. Why is hope so prevalent in every aspect of our life?

Maybe you, like me, have had the following experience: you are up until 3 am studying for your math exam in the morning. Your alarm goes off. Tired and half asleep, you get up as quickly as possible. As you are getting ready, you keep telling yourself over and over that you hope you remember everything you have learned for the test. As you were about to leave, you check your phone and you have received a text message from your best friend saying, 'I hope you're doing well today. All the best in your exam.' You quickly reply, 'I'm doing well, thank you. This test is my only hope to get an A in the class. I feel prepared for it. Anyway, I hope you have a good day today as well.' You go to the exam center, nervous but with great hopes of passing the exam. After an hour of work, you've finished your exam. You get out and check your phone and you have seven missed calls and one voicemail from your mom. As you were about to text her, your phone starts ringing again, and it is your mom calling.

You pick it up and her first words were, 'Hello sweetie, I hope your exam went well.' 'It did, thank you Mom,' you reply. You talk for a few minutes and you said goodbye. After the call, your friend comes running up and taps you on the shoulder and says, 'I hope we passed the exam. The questions were a little tricky.' 'Yeah, I hope so too,' you reply.

The word, hope, has become part of our everyday vocabulary, especially as we live in a world of great pressure and expectation to succeed.

What is Hope?

Hope is the thing with feathers that perches in the soul and sings the tune without the words—and never stops at all—Emily Dickinson

The Hebrew root verb 'qa-wah', from which come terms rendered 'hope,' basically means 'wait for with eager expectation'. The Merriam-Webster Dictionary defines hope in the noun and verb form. The definition of hope in the noun form is: 'to cherish with anticipation; to want something to happen or be true'. For example, to hope for a promotion or hoping for the best. The definition of hope in the verb form according to the dictionary is: 'to desire with expectation of obtainment or fulfillment with confidence'. For example, I hope she remembers, or I hope your mother is doing well. Never give up!

We all face challenges in life that affect our self-esteem, tarnish our confidence, increase anxiety, and change the way we see the world. These challenges—ranging from poverty, poor health, the death of loved ones, addiction, and among many others—determine our hope. Hope is not just a feeling of expectation, but an innate ability to do our best to improve the challenges we face. Hope is about changing our mindset, our attitude, and having the belief that things will improve. When we work hard, when we are honest, when we help others in need, we display our desire to bring hope. This book is a story of how our desire to serve others can help improve the mindset and attitude of people to bring them to hope in the face of adversity.

My story. Your story. Our story! We all have a unique story to tell, to inspire others, and to be inspired in return. Our past struggles and present successes shape the stories we share. We perceive the world through different lenses, based on the culture, family, and environment we are born into. No matter which lenses we use, we need to make sure our words, choices, and actions bring positive change in our lives and the people around us. There are many problems in this world, yet we wake up every day and follow the same routine of school, work, and family. Humanity has seen a lot of changes, from the primitive style living of cavemen to the advanced age of technology. Yet humanity's desire to bring change has not been met with the problems it faces. Wars, diseases, the death of loved ones and many natural disasters have inspired mankind to find answers to life's misery and the desire to live forever. We give money to charity because we want things to change. We want things to improve, not stay the same.

Somewhere in the depths of our hearts, we have a desire to make a difference. We all want our lives to have a significance in society. In an often-dreary world, each dollar we give to charity is a sign that we have not yet lost hope in humanity. In the middle of our busy lives, each contribution is a sign that we have not forgotten about all those who live in abject poverty, despair, and abandonment.

Out of this basic giving desire within us has grown a charity outside of us—a multibillion-dollar industry employing millions of people who work to turn our contributions to effect positive change. We put our trust not just in individual charities, but in the system of charity itself to take our contributions and make them a better world. However, the non-profit organisations we believe in and offer our contributions to don't seem to be giving us the changes we want to see in this world—peace, love, unity, and happiness.

So, we constantly ask ourselves, why do things stay the same? Why have our cancer research charities not discovered a cure for cancer? Why have our homeless shelters not solved the problem of homelessness? Why do children in Africa and other parts of the world still go to bed hungry? Why have refugee children pictures not changed in the last ten decades? Why, in this age of incredible affluence and advanced technology, do we seem unable to close the gaps that divide those who live in comfort and those who suffer?

This persistent desire for a better tomorrow is the seed of our hope and it boils deep within our heart. It moves every fiber of our body to make that hope come alive. Our stories stem from the hope we have in bringing a change to ourselves, to our families, to our environment, and to the world in general. Growing up in the environment I found myself, not by choice, as none of us choose which family or environment we are born into. I realized that everyone has the potential to hope for a better future. Whether we are rich or poor, whether young or old, we all have something we hope to have or something we hope to improve or change in our lives.

It is important to appreciate what we have and hope for something better for ourselves and others. Transforming hope into reality takes time and effort. We need hard work to stay focused, we need the patience to have soundness of mind, and we also need peace for appreciation of life because of the hope we have. What is the purpose of life? Why are we here? Where do we go after death? Is this what life is all about? All these questions come to our mind and help us to reflect on ourselves and what we can do to bring fulfillment to our lives and that of others. Each day needs to add meaning to our life, and to the hope we have.

References:

i   Everyone has the Right to Dream. Retrieved from Right to Dream Academy - https://www.righttodream.com

ii   Feyenord Academy. Retrieved from Feyenord Football Club Academy - https://www.feyenoord.com/youth-academy/about-academy

iii   Fulham Academy. Retrieved from Fulham Football Club Academy- https://www.fulhamfc.com/the-teams/academy

iv   Peak. Performance. Project. Retrieved from P3 - http://www.p3.md/

v   Paleta, S. (2012, April). The Next Great Philanthropist (Video file). Retrieved https://youtu.be/BrT3VQwwlek

vi   Santa Barbara Newspaper. Retrieved from KEYT- https://www.keyt.com/sports/former-gaucho-soccer-star-has-set-a-big-goal-of-helping-children-in-ghana/761135261

vii   Greenleaf, R. K. (1970). The servant as leader. Cambridge, Mass: Center for Applied Studies.

viii   http://www.nigeria-law.org/Criminal%20Code%20Act-Part%20VI%20%20to%20the%20end.htm

ix   Preventive research. Retrieved from Salovey, P., Rothman, A. J., Detweiler, J. B., & Steward, W. T. (2000). Emotional states and physical health. American Psychologist, 55, 110- 121.

x   Taylor et al., 2000. Psychological resources, positive illusions, and health. American Psychologist, 55, 99-109.

CPSIA information can be obtained
at www.ICGtesting.com
Printed in the USA
FSHW021249041019
62701FS